Module 10

Reading Big W
Syllabication and Advanced Decoding

LETRS

Language Essentials
for Teachers of
Reading and
Spelling

Louisa C. Moats, Ed.D.

SOPRIS WEST EDUCATIONAL SERVICES
A CAMBIUM LEARNING COMPANY

BOSTON, MA • NEW YORK, NY • LONGMONT, CO

ISBN 1-59318-198-1

Printed in the United States of America

Published and Distributed by

Sopris West™
EDUCATIONAL SERVICES

A Cambium Learning Company

4093 Specialty Place • Longmont, CO 80504 • (303) 651-2829
www.sopriswest.com

191MOD10/6-06

Dedication

For Steve, without whom my work would be impossible,
and with whom I have joy in every day.

Acknowledgments

Only with the contributions of many people can a project such as LETRS be realized. At Sopris West Educational Services, I am grateful to Toni Backstrom, Tyra Segars, Sue Campbell, Lynne Stair, Christine Kosmicki, Sherri Rowe, Kim Harris, Karen Butler, and Sandra Knauke for their work on LETRS programs and publications. Michelle LaBorde and John Morris-Riehl have contributed extraordinary talent and dedication to development of the LETRS CD-ROMs.

The national LETRS trainers and consultants are invaluable guides and companions in this endeavor. They include Carol Tolman, Anne Cunningham, Marcia Davidson, Deb Glaser, Marsha Berger, Linda Farrell, Susan Hall, Judi Dodson, Anne Whitney, Nancy Hennessy, Mary Dahlgren, and Susan Smartt. I am grateful to many others who have attended institutes, offered suggestions, and shaped the content and activities in LETRS.

Stuart Horsfall, Chet Foraker, Steve Kukic, and Steve Mitchell at Sopris West Educational Services have given this project enthusiastic support from the beginning. I am deeply indebted to you for your commitment to content-rich professional development.

About the Author

Louisa C. Moats, Ed.D., is a nationally recognized authority on how children learn to read and why people fail to learn to read. Widely acclaimed as a researcher, speaker, consultant, and trainer, Dr. Moats has developed the landmark professional development program LETRS for teachers and reading specialists. Between 1997 and 2001 she completed four years as site director of the NICHD Early Interventions Project in Washington, D.C., which included daily work with inner-city teachers and children. This longitudinal, large-scale project was conducted through the University of Texas, Houston; it investigated the causes and remedies for reading failure in high-poverty urban schools. Dr. Moats spent the previous 15 years in private practice as a licensed psychologist in Vermont, specializing in evaluation and consultation with individuals of all ages who experienced difficulty with reading, spelling, writing, and oral language.

Dr. Moats began her professional career as a neuropsychology technician and teacher of students with learning disabilities. She later earned her master's degree at Peabody College of Vanderbilt University and her doctorate in reading and human development from the Harvard Graduate School of Education. She has been licensed to teach in three states. Louisa has been an adjunct professor of psychiatry at Dartmouth Medical School and clinical associate professor of pediatrics at the University of Texas at Houston.

In addition to LETRS, Modules 1–9 (Sopris West Educational Services, 2005), her authored and coauthored books include:

- *Speech to Print: Language Essentials for Teachers* (Paul Brookes Publishing, 2000)

- *Spelling: Development, Disability, and Instruction* (York Press, 1995)

- *Straight Talk About Reading* (Contemporary Books, 1998)

- *Parenting a Struggling Reader* (Random House, 2002)

- *Spellography* (Sopris West Educational Services, 2002)

Louisa has also published numerous journal articles, chapters, and policy papers including: the American Federation of Teachers' "Teaching Reading is Rocket Science"; the Learning First Alliance's "Every Child Reading: A Professional Development Guide"; and—with Barbara Foorman—the report on the D.C. Early Interventions Project: "Conditions for Sustaining Research-Based Practices in Early Reading Instruction" (*Journal of Remedial and Special Education*, 2004). She continues to dedicate her professional work to the improvement of teacher preparation and professional development. She is the consulting director of literacy research and professional development for Sopris West Educational Services.

Louisa and her husband divide their time among homes in Colorado, Idaho, and Vermont. Their extended family includes a professional skier, a school psychologist, an alpaca rancher, and an Australian shepherd.

Contents for Module 10

Overview of LETRS: Language Essentials for Teachers of Reading and Spelling

LETRS is a series of professional development modules for teachers of reading, spelling, and writing—including general and special educators—that:

◆ Teaches in depth the theory and practice of "scientifically based reading instruction."

◆ Fosters insight into *why* specific instructional practices are effective and *how* to implement them.

◆ Engages teachers in a rewarding, informative learning experience.

Content of LETRS Modules Within the Language-Literacy Connection

The content and activities in LETRS help teachers understand:

◆ How students learn to read and write.

◆ The reasons why some children fail to learn.

◆ The instructional strategies best supported by research.

As author of the American Federation of Teachers' "Teaching Reading *Is* Rocket Science" and the Learning First Alliance's "Every Child Reading: A Professional Development Guide"—as well as contributor to the Reading First Leadership Academies—Dr. Moats has used these works and contributions as blueprints for LETRS. The use of LETRS in professional development associated with Reading First and other reading initiatives is now widespread.

The format of LETRS instruction allows for greater depth of learning and reflection than the brief "once-over" treatment these topics are typically given in professional development. Modules are designed for:

◆ Teachers who are in pre-service licensing programs.

◆ Teachers who are implementing a core, comprehensive reading instruction program or an intervention program.

♦ Coaches, mentors, and course instructors who wish to better understand the foundation concepts of effective teaching practices in reading, spelling, and writing.

Users of this material are encouraged to read widely from the list of teacher resources and instructional programs and references in this module, as well as seek out important summary documents, books, and journal articles on reading psychology and research-based reading instruction.

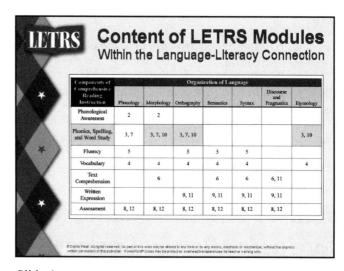

Slide 1

Goal for Module 10

To prepare teachers of students (grade 3 and above) to build upon a foundation of phonics with a structured system of word study and advanced decoding.

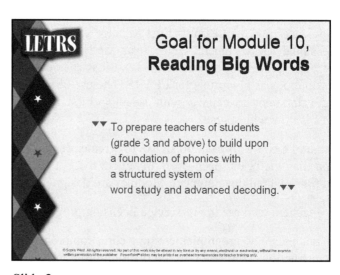

Slide 2

Objectives

◆ Evaluate one's own knowledge of word structure with the Pretest and Posttest.

◆ Understand and articulate the value of teaching word structure and decoding skills in grade 3 and beyond.

◆ Review what there is to teach, by grade level, with reference to the historical "layer cake" of English (Anglo-Saxon, Norman French, Latin, Greek).

◆ Map phonemes to graphemes in single-syllable words.

◆ Identify, categorize, and combine six predictable syllable structures in written English, and recognize exceptions to these categories.

◆ Divide multisyllabic words using several high-utility principles.

◆ Sort past-tense and plural words by the sounds of those inflections, and understand why those alternations occur.

◆ Review a lesson framework for teaching recognition of big words.

◆ Explore word families derived from a common root.

◆ Identify stable prefixes and changeable ("chameleon") prefixes.

◆ Alter a word's grammatical role by changing the suffix.

◆ Review and role-play a lesson routine for teaching syllabication and morphology.

LETRS

The Component in Focus, Module 10

- Phonological and Phoneme Awareness
- **Phonics and Word Study**
- Reading Fluency
- Vocabulary
- Text Comprehension
  - speaking and listening
  - written expression

Slide 3

Pretest: Survey of Word Knowledge for Teachers

Answer the questions on this survey to see how much you already know about the structure of English words. We expect you to be unsure of some answers; that's why this module was written! You'll do the survey again once the module is completed.

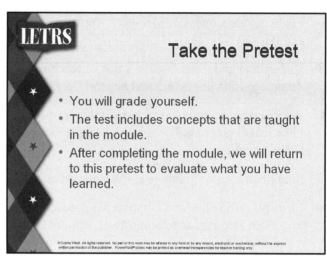

Slide 4

1. Identify the letter groups that correspond to each of the speech sounds in the following words. Circle each letter or letter group (grapheme) that corresponds to a speech sound (phoneme).

   birch   straight   watch   scrabble   cleave   destroy

2. Divide each of these words into syllables, using syllable division principles to guide pronunciation.

   cooperate   unremitting   comedy   vaccination

   poetry   panorama   slugger   impersonal

3. Sort these words into one of three groups: those that appear to come from Old English (Anglo-Saxon), those that come from Latin, and those that come from Greek. (Label each word AS, L, or Gr on the line before the word.)

   _____ water   _____ omnivore   _____ aquarium   _____ irrigation

   _____ submersion   _____ chlorophyll   _____ bread   _____ drought

4. Explain the spelling convention that is illustrated by each double-letter pattern in the following words:

   a. **floss** _____

   b. **flapped** _____

   c. **commit** _____

   d. **illiterate** _____

Why Teach Decoding and Word Structure to Older Students?

Reading: A National Challenge At Every Age

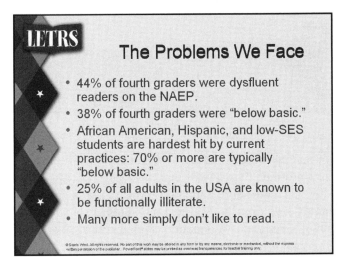

The Problems We Face

- 44% of fourth graders were dysfluent readers on the NAEP.
- 38% of fourth graders were "below basic."
- African American, Hispanic, and low-SES students are hardest hit by current practices: 70% or more are typically "below basic."
- 25% of all adults in the USA are known to be functionally illiterate.
- Many more simply don't like to read.

Slide 5

The social and economic consequences of reading failure are far-reaching and have been labeled a major public health issue by the National Institutes of Health (NIH). According to the National Assessment of Educational Progress (NAEP)—the only measure that allows this nation to compare reading achievement across states—44% of all fourth graders are dysfluent readers, and about 38% score "below basic" on passage-reading tests. In high-poverty areas serving Hispanic and African American children, the percentage of children who are poor readers is much higher.

Dysfluent readers are hesitant and slow; they labor over the words and often have little idea about what they are reading. In real life, they are averse to reading because reading is effortful, inaccurate, and slow. Beyond first and second grade—after children should have learned how to read—those students who are below the average range often find themselves unable to participate fully in their schooling. Poor reading is likely to affect them for life. In fact, 25% of adults in the United States are functionally illiterate; many more just don't like to read.

LETRS Consensus Findings From Rigorous, Scientific Reading Research ...

- Report of the National Reading Panel
- Summary reports by the National Institutes of Health, the National Institute for Literacy, and the Partnership for Reading
- American Federation of Teachers' special publications on reading instruction
- The Learning First Alliance
- The American Psychological Society's monograph (2001)
- The National Academy of Sciences, PRF
- The Society for the Scientific Study of Reading

Slide 6

Research in reading development and reading difficulty has been extensive and has been informed by many disciplines—psychology, genetics, neurology, linguistics, and education. Funding for this research has been provided by various sources, including the National Institutes of Health, the United States Department of Education, foundations, universities, and business groups. Consensus on major issues regarding reading development and instruction is so strong (National Institute of Child Health and Human Development, 2000; Rayner, Foorman, Perfetti, Pesetsky, & Seidenberg, 2001; Stanovich, 2001) that federal, state, and district programs and policies are requiring instruction to be "research-based."

Long-term studies clearly show that once children fall behind in reading, they seldom catch up unless they receive specialized, intensive instruction (Juel, 1994; Fletcher & Lyon, 1998; Torgesen et al., 2001). Children of poverty and children in minority groups fare much more poorly in reading than white, middle- or upper-income children. In spite of that discouraging reality, research has also shown that low-achieving children can be brought to at least the national average or beyond (Foorman et al., 2003; Torgesen et al., 2001), even in the intermediate and middle grades (Curtis, 2002; Archer, Gleason, & Vachon, 2003).

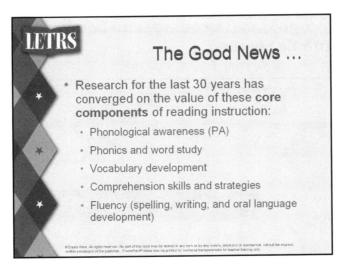

Slide 7

What should we do to help older, poor readers close the gap and read at grade level? First, we should assume that reading is an acquired skill that can be taught to students of any age. Even non-literate adults can learn to read. Early intervention works best, but it is never too late to help older, poor readers (Berninger et al., 2003; Moats, 2001; Rashotte, MacPhee, & Torgesen, 2001; Torgesen, Rashotte, Alexander, Alexander, & MacPhee, 2003).

The components of effective programs for older, poor readers include the components that have been proven necessary for younger, novice readers; the emphasis and content of instruction, however, may vary. Effective programs for poor readers include systematic, explicit, structured, sequential teaching of phonological awareness, phonics, and word analysis, coupled with explicit teaching of reading fluency, vocabulary, and comprehension. Writing skills should be integrated with all of these components, as well. Of course, the emphasis of instruction will vary according the student's level of reading skill, as measured by accuracy and speed of oral reading and silent passage reading.

Word Recognition (Decoding) and Comprehension Must Both Be Learned

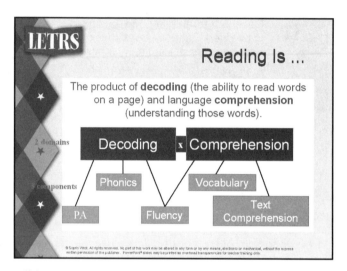

Slide 8

Two major domains of knowledge and skill must be developed in order for children to read well (Gough, Juel, & Griffith, 1992). One domain, usually referred to as **decoding** or **word recognition**, involves instant recognition of printed words—naming the words on the page with sufficient speed to support comprehension. The other domain, usually referred to as **comprehension** ability, involves knowledge of word and phrase meanings, interpretation of sentences, construction of the main ideas, making connections between what is read with prior knowledge of the world, and deployment of strategies to clarify and remember the content. This model suggests that students may have relative strengths and weaknesses in decoding, comprehension, or both.

Slide 9

Four possible types of students:

Good decoding, weak comprehension (About 10% of poor readers)	Good decoding, good comprehension (Majority of good readers)
Poor decoding, poor comprehension (Majority of poor readers)	Poor decoding, good comprehension (About 20% of poor readers)

Many well-designed research studies strongly indicate that learning to decode and learning to comprehend go hand-in-hand. The large majority of students who struggle with reading fall behind early (in first grade) because they are having trouble with the basics: letter recognition, speech-sound awareness (phonemic awareness), sound-letter correspondence (phonics), and fluent word recognition. Some may be accurate in decoding but lack the speed or fluency of word recognition that permits comprehension. A few students are accurate and fluent in reading the words but are weak in understanding what they are reading; research suggests that these students compose about 10% of poor readers (Shankweiler et al., 1995; Shankweiler, Lundquist, Dreyer, & Dickinson, 1996; Shankweiler et al., 1999).

In general, accurate and fluent reading for meaning goes with strong word-recognition skills (for reviews, see Adams, Treiman, & Pressley, 1997; Rayner et al., 2001; Share & Stanovich, 1995), and word recognition itself depends on both awareness of the speech sounds in words (phonological awareness) and awareness of the exact letter sequences in words (orthographic processing) (Ehri, 1998).

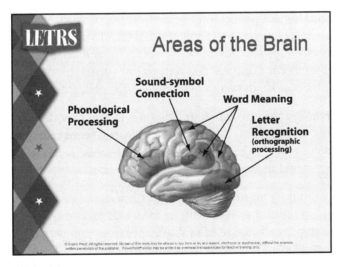

Slide 10

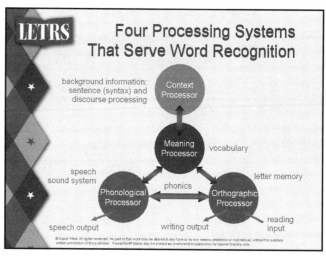

Slide 11

Phonological processing and **orthographic processing** may be new terms for teachers, but they are important to understand because they direct us toward instructional solutions. Good readers know the individual sounds (phonemes) in the word and the letter sequence that represents the word in print. They are aware of the details of both speech and print, and they know how to match speech sounds (phonemes) with letters and letter sequences (graphemes). The "four-part processing model" that we have explored in other LETRS modules—derived from cognitive sciences and neurosciences (Eden & Moats, 2002; Rayner et al., 2001)—suggests that sounds, letters, word meanings, and the context in which a word occurs all are processed accurately and efficiently during skilled reading. Thus, the job of the teacher will be to educate all of these processing systems thoroughly and systematically.

What the processing systems do to recognize words:

◆ **Phonological processing:** Identification, production, and manipulation of speech sounds, spoken syllables, rhyme patterns, and prosody (ups and downs of the voice, as well as stress patterns within words); storage and retrieval of verbal information; memory for the sounds in names and new words; phoneme awareness.

◆ **Orthographic processing:** Attention to letter sequences and patterns; memory for "sight" words or instant word recognition; differentiation of similar-looking letters and words; recall of letters that correspond to speech sounds.

◆ **Meaning (semantic) processing:** Connection of the spoken and written form of a word with its meaning; recognition of word relationships; knowledge of multiple meanings and uses of words and phrases.

◆ **Context (syntactic and discourse) processing:** Constructing a word's meaning from the sentence and passage context in which it occurs.

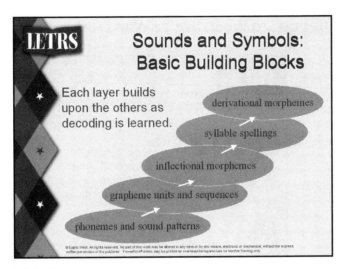

Slide 12

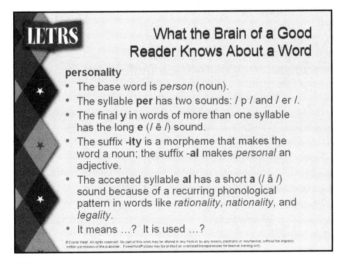

Slide 13

Exercise #1: What Kinds of Knowledge Do We Bring to Word Recognition?

◆ Read the novel words in this passage as well as you can:

To stabilize the pretractal fordex, the brave engineer resituated the gyrine. Then he tribled the cabulum.

"Oh, whippers!" he exclaimed. "Thank heavens, I'm no longer befuddled by this problem."

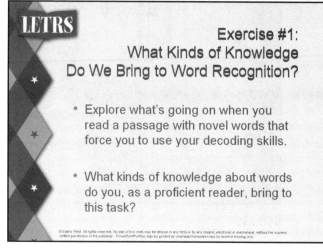

Slide 14

◆ Answer these questions:

1. What is the root of the word *pretractal*? How many meaningful parts (morphemes) are there in that word?

   _____

   _____

2. Where is the syllable stress or accent in the word *pretractal*? Why?

   _____

   _____

3. How did you pronounce the first **t** in the word *resituated*? Why?

   _____

   _____

   _____

4. How did you pronounce the word *gyrine*? What other known word might you be comparing it to?

   _____

   _____

   _____

Exercise #1 *(continued)*

5. Is the vowel in the first syllable of the word *tribled* long or short? Why?

_____

_____

_____

6. Where is the accent on the word *befuddled*? Why?

_____

_____

7. What kind of word (i.e., part of speech) is *cabulum*? How do you know?

_____

_____

8. Is the first vowel in the word *whippers* long or short? Why?

_____

_____

_____

◆ **Discussion:** Consider the various types of word knowledge that allowed you to read the words in this passage. Can you find an instance in which you:

- Made a letter-sound (grapheme-phoneme) association?

  _____

- Made an analogy between the word parts and patterns of the new word with those of a known word?

  _____

- Divided a word into common meaningful parts (morphemes)?

  _____

- Applied syllable division conventions to decide how to pronounce a vowel?

  _____

- Recognized a familiar whole word by sight?

  _____

All of these approaches to word recognition operate in the mind of a skilled reader! Children eventually learn to read by incrementally gaining skill with sounds, letter patterns, meaningful parts of words, syllable division, and whole-word recognition.

Again, national data show that 4 out of 10 children in a typical third and fourth grade will be slow and/or inaccurate in word-reading skills! In some schools, the percentage is higher. Many of those students also need to work on fluency, vocabulary, and comprehension strategies. However, *comprehension improvement is often contingent upon students learning how to read the words accurately and fluently*. Intermediate, middle school, high school, and adult students who do not decode with fluency and flexibility will need direct teaching of phonics and word analysis within a comprehensive approach.

Children who can read the words accurately and fluently also will benefit from studying the structure of words, although they may need less practice than their struggling classmates and can work at a more advanced level. Their spelling will improve if they understand the origin and meanings of words in relation to the print. If older, poor readers have never established phoneme awareness, they may need instruction that rebuilds this important foundation.

Recent studies of the language knowledge of teachers indicate that most of us need to study the speech sounds, the spelling system, and the structure of words before we feel comfortable teaching the material to students. When we do know the content of advanced phonics ourselves, however, instruction can be active, fun, and engaging for both teacher and students.

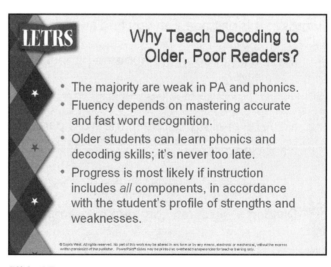

Slide 15

To summarize, word decoding (phonics and more) and word study are necessary for teaching older, poor readers because:

◆ Most poor readers failed to acquire sufficient skill in phonemic awareness, phonics, and word recognition in the beginning stages of reading.

◆ Comprehension depends on fluent, accurate word recognition.

◆ It is never too late! Basic reading skills can be learned by older students—including adults—if instruction is systematic, explicit, cumulative, and comprehensive.

◆ Scientifically validated instructional programs include a strong component on word recognition, as well as fluency, vocabulary, and comprehension.

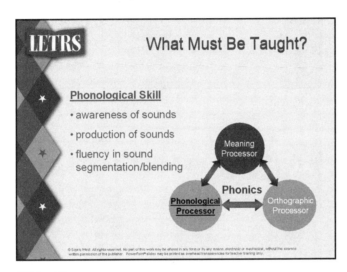

Slide 16

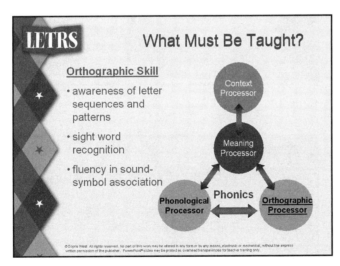

Slide 17

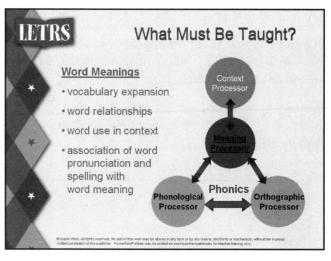

Slide 18

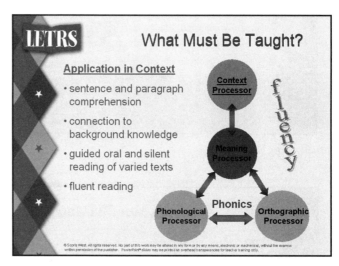

Slide 19

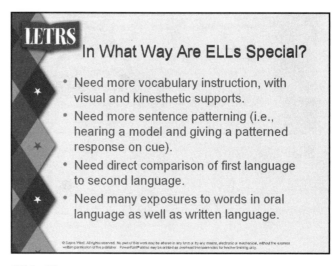

Slide 20

What to Teach in Advanced Phonics and Word Study

Word Study Can Be Organized According to the Historical Layers of English

Why is English a more difficult language to spell and decode than other European languages such as Spanish, Italian, Serbo-Croatian, or Finnish? Because it embodies several languages! English is a "polyglot" language, a linguistic layer cake constructed through centuries of English history (Henry, 2003; King, 2000). Consider the words in these expressions of affection:

> If music be the food of love, play on.

> I am infatuated with my admirer.

> My fiancé is gentile.

> I felt platonic love and sympathy for the ailing patriarch.

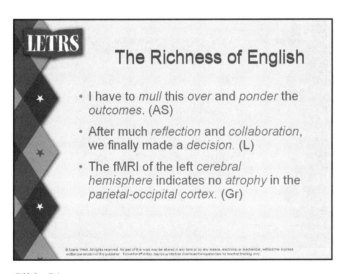

Slide 21

Several parent languages are represented in this vocabulary. The ancestor of Modern English is Anglo-Saxon (Old English), the Germanic tongue of Norse tribesmen who populated the British Isles before A.D. 1066. After the invasion by Norman French armies and William the Conqueror, the language of the Norse French—a close cousin to Latin—was imposed on British natives for almost 400 years. Old French (Norman French) and Old English (Anglo-Saxon) were gradually amalgamated, merging into Middle English by the late 15th century. With the advent of the printing press in the early 1500s, more and more written material was generated and consumed, and standard-ization of vocabulary and spelling began to occur. Scholars trained in the clas-sics coined thousands of words in the 16th and 17th centuries, many based on

Latin roots and spelled with borrowed patterns. As scientific discoveries multiplied during the Renaissance, scholars also coined terms from Greek for new scientific and mathematical ideas, a convention that continues today.

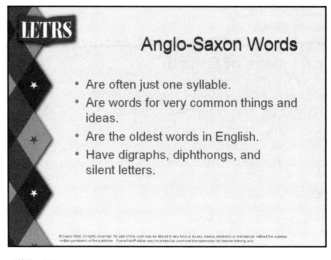

Slide 22

Slide 23

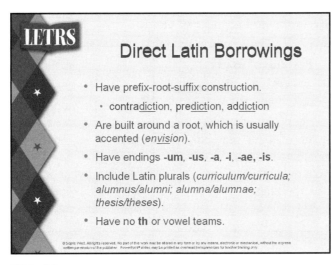

Slide 24

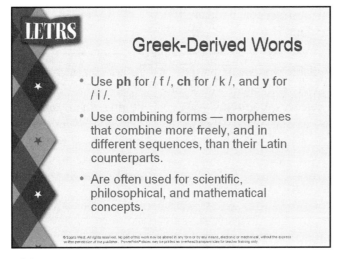

Slide 25

Table 10.1 Characteristics of English Words According to Language of Origin

Language of Origin	Features of Words	Examples
Anglo-Saxon (Old English)	Short, one syllable; sometimes compounded; use of vowel teams, silent letters, digraphs, diphthongs in spelling; words for common, everyday things; irregular spellings	*sky, earth, moon, sun, water sheep, dog, horse, cow, hen head, arm, finger, toe, heart shoe, shirt, pants, socks, coat brother, father, mother, sister hate, love, think, want, touch does, were, been, would, do*
Norman French	**ou** for / u /; soft **c** and **g** when followed by **e, i, y**; special endings such as **-ine, -ette, -elle, -ique**; words for food and fashion, abstract social ideals, relationships	*amuse, cousin, cuisine, country, peace, triage, rouge, baguette, novice, justice, soup, coupon, nouvelle, boutique*
Latin/Romance	Multisyllabic words with prefixes, roots, suffixes; content words for social sciences, traditional physical sciences, and literature	*firmament, terrestrial, solar, stellar, aquarium, mammal, equine, pacify, mandible, extremity, locomotion, paternal, maternity, designate, hostility, amorous, contemplate, delectable, deception, reject, refer*
Greek	Spellings **ph** for / f /, **ch** for / k /, and **y** for / ĭ /; constructed from combining forms, similar to English compounds; scientific, philosophical, and mathematical terminology	*hypnosis, agnostic, neuropsychology, decathalon, catatonic, agoraphobia, chlorophyll, physiognomy*

Exercise #2: Finding Anglo-Saxon, Latin, and Greek in English

- ◆ Combine these word parts to make as many new words as you can in the table below.

- ◆ Then decide what language each word probably came from. Use a dictionary if you need to.

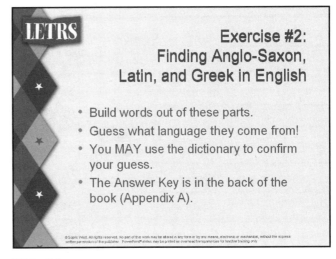

Slide 26

graph	-ology	dog	phon(e) / phono	audi	xylo	-ed
say	-tory	cep	ear	per		
-tion	shot	listen	-er	hear		

Anglo-Saxon (AS) (Old English)	Latin (L) (Romance)	Greek (Gr)
_____	_____	_____
_____	_____	_____
_____	_____	_____
_____	_____	_____
_____	_____	_____
_____	_____	_____
_____	_____	_____
_____	_____	_____
_____	_____	_____

Why Is Awareness of Word Origin Helpful?

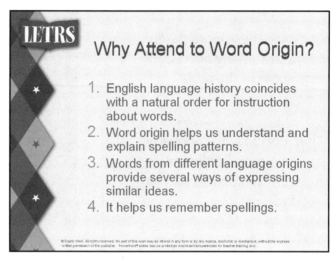

Slide 27

1. To provide a rationale for the order and emphasis of instruction about words.

   • Phonics begins with the sound-symbol correspondences characteristic of the base layer of English—Anglo-Saxon. It progresses through syllable patterns, compounds, contractions, and inflected endings, all Anglo-Saxon. Word study continues with Latin and Greek derivatives and word-building in the intermediate grades.

2. To explain spellings that appear to be odd or irregular.

   • The words *Aphrodite, catastrophe, anemone,* and *apostrophe* have the letter **e** on the end because use of the letter **e** for the long / ē / sound is derived from Greek spelling. In Anglo-Saxon and Latin words, a final-**e** syllable is usually spelled with the letter **y** (e.g., *baby, squishy, antipathy, infinity*).

   The word *irregular* is spelled with two **r**'s because it is composed of a Latin prefix (**ir-** / **in-**) and a root (*regular*), whereas the word *iridescence* comes from the Greek root, *iri*, meaning "a play of colors."

   The words *antique, unique, opaque, mystique,* and *oblique* are perfectly regular in French.

3. To expand vocabulary by finding alternate words for similar ideas. (AS = Anglo-Saxon; L = Latin; NF = Norman French; Gr = Greek; Ger = German)

   alive (AS), *thriving* (AS), *animate* (L), *spirited* (L)

   sad (AS), *depressed* (L), *morose* (NF), *catatonic* (Gr)

   talkative (AS), *garrulous* (L), *verbose* (NF/L)

   dead (AS), *deceased* (NF), *moribund* (L), *kaput* (Ger)

4. To help us remember how to spell.

    Ante means "before" in Latin, so an *antecedent* comes before something else; this prefix is also related to the words *antebellum* and *antedate*.

    Anti means "against" in Latin, so *antidemocratic* means against democratic principles; an *antidepressant* works against depression; and *antipathy* is a strong feeling against an ideal, value, or topic.

    The word *antique* is French; it's a combination of the Latin *ante* for "before" and the French ending **-ique**. The word *ant* has nothing to do with either one of these meanings! It's Anglo-Saxon.

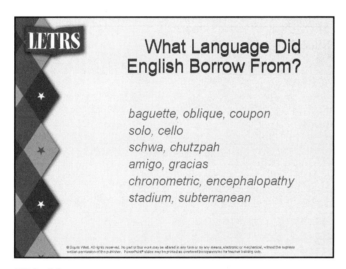

Slide 28

The Progression of Word Study Instruction

The content of word study, then, can be envisioned as a progression from the study of single-syllable Anglo-Saxon words and their sound-symbol correspondences to the study of syllables and morphemes (meaningful parts) in Anglo-Saxon words of more than one syllable. Next come words of Latin and Old French (Norman-French) origin, emphasized in the intermediate grades when children are progressing on grade level (Henry, 2003). Finally, the Greek layer of language becomes grist for the word study mill, comprising terms needed in science, mathematics, and philosophy.

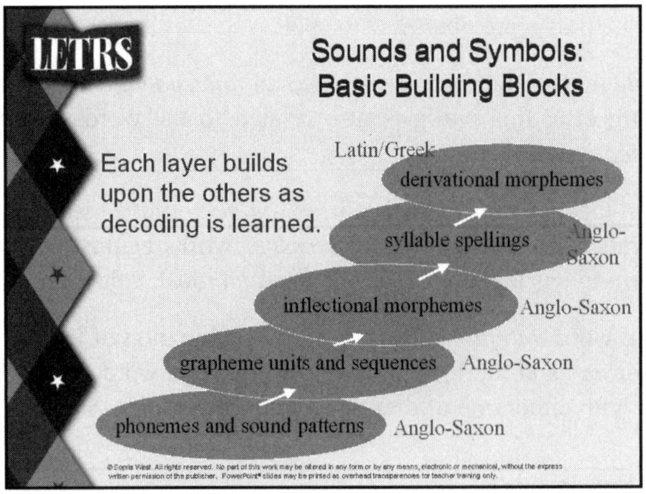
LETRS
Sounds and Symbols: Basic Building Blocks
Each layer builds upon the others as decoding is learned.
Latin/Greek
derivational morphemes
syllable spellings
Anglo-Saxon
inflectional morphemes
Anglo-Saxon
grapheme units and sequences
Anglo-Saxon
phonemes and sound patterns
Anglo-Saxon

Slide 29

Table 10.2 Progression of Word Study Through Grades 1–8

Historical Layers of English	Sound-Symbol Correspondence	Syllable Patterns	Morpheme Structures

Anglo-Saxon Layer (Grades 1–3)	Consonants
	  – single
	  – digraphs
	  – blends
	Vowels
	  – single short/long
	  – VC-**e**
	  – vowel team
	  – vowel-**r** patterns
		1. Closed (short **v**)
		2. Open (single long **v**)
		3. Magic-**e** (VC-**e**)
		4. Vowel-**r**
		5. Vowel team
		6. Consonant-**le**
		7. Oddities
			Compounds (*daylight*)
			
			Inflections (**-ed, -s, -es, -er, est, -ing**)
			
			Base words
			
			Suffixes (**-en, -hood, -ly, -ward**)
			
			Odd, high-frequency words (*said, does*)

Old French	**ch** for / sh / (*chaperone*)
	ou for / ū / (*soup, journey*)
	que for / k / (*opaque*)
	qu for / kw / (*queen*)
	c for / s / (*residence*)
	g for / j / (*gentle*)
		(various borrowings)
		  -ette
		  -ique
		  -ile	

Latin (Romance Layer) (Grades 4–6)			Prefixes (**pre-, inter-**) Roots (**gress, ject, vis**) Suffixes (**-ment, -ity**) Latin plurals (*alumni, minutiae, curricula*)

Greek Layer (Grades 6–8)	Spellings:
	  ph for / f / (*graph*)
	  ch for / k / (*chorus*)
	  y for / ĭ / (*gym*)
			Combining forms:
			  neuro
			  psych
			  ology
			  lex
			  chloro
			
			Plurals (*crises, metamorphoses*)

Anglo-Saxon Sounds and Symbols: The Building Blocks of Syllables

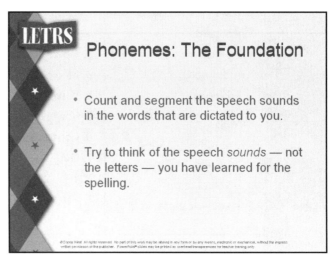

Slide 30

Phonemes

A **phoneme** is an individual speech sound in the language. Other words that use the root **phone** are telephone, *phonograph*, *phonology*, *megaphone*, *microphone*, *phonics*, *symphony*, and *xylophone*. The English language has 43 phonemes—25 consonants and 18 vowels (see Appendix D for the speech sounds charts)[1]. Listen while the presenter asks you to segment the speech sounds in words he/she pronounces for you.

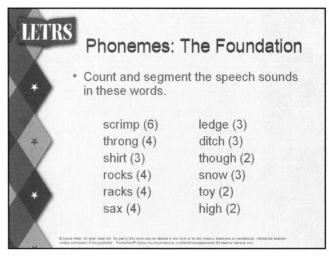

Slide 31

[1] Linguists do not agree on how many speech sounds there are in English, so you may know a different way of classifying the phonemes.

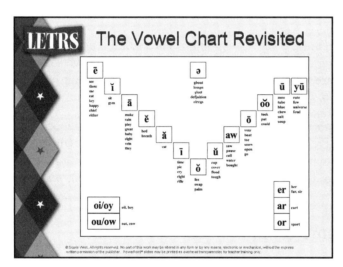

Slide 32

Slide 33

Graphemes

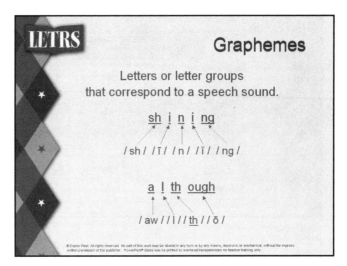

Slide 34

A **grapheme** is a letter or group of letters that represents one speech sound. A grapheme may be one letter (the **b** in *battle*), two letters (**th** and **ng** in *thing*), three letters (**igh** in *fight*; **dge** in *dodge*), or four letters (**eigh** in *eight*; **ough** in *though*).

A **digraph** is a two-letter consonant spelling for a unique speech sound that is not represented by either letter (e.g., **th**, **sh**, **ch**, **wh**, **ng**, **ph**, **gh**). Most speech sounds in English spelling are represented with more than one letter. Other words that use the root **graph** are *phonograph, photograph, digraph, biography, telegraph, autograph, graphic,* and *polygraph.*

Phoneme-Grapheme Correspondence

The majority of older, struggling readers have not learned well enough how to decode a new, unfamiliar word. They may know very elementary phonics but may not be accurate or fast at dividing longer words, identifying the vowel sound, or blending words together. Unless they learn to decode proficiently, they will be slow and inaccurate in text reading, thereby missing many of the most important content words in their reading. Their weak decoding skills may be evident even in one-syllable words. If students are not proficient at linking letters to speech sounds, reading one-syllable words, or writing a good phonetic equivalent for an unknown word, they probably need to review basic sound-symbol correspondences in common Anglo-Saxon syllable patterns (Archer et al., 2003; Ehri & Soffer, 1999; Scheerer-Neumann, 1981).

Phoneme-Grapheme Mapping (PGM)

LETRS
Phoneme-Grapheme Mapping (PGM)

- A technique for teaching sound-letter correspondences that is multisensory and engaging.
- The link that good readers make between speech and print.

Slide 35

Phoneme-grapheme mapping (Grace, in press) is an active, enjoyable approach to teaching students about the sounds (**phonemes**) in words and the letters (**graphemes**) that represent them.[2] PGM is an exercise that requires students to attend to the internal details of words and to understand how letters are used to represent each of the speech sounds. This awareness, in turn, helps students remember words for reading, spelling, and vocabulary. When students develop insight into word structure and the ability to think about words—or **metalinguistic awareness**—their reading, spelling, and use of words will improve.

LETRS
Prerequisite Student Skills for PGM

1. Can give individual speech sounds for consonants and digraphs.
2. Can blend three phonemes to make a word.
3. Can substitute a single sound to make a new word.
4. Can segment words into three sounds.
5. With cues, can identify a short vowel sound in a word.
6. Can name all letters.
7. Can read 50–100 words "by sight."

Slide 36

---

[2] *Reading Big Words: Syllabication and Advanced Decoding* Procedures for phoneme-grapheme mapping are based on Kathi Grace's forthcoming manual, to be published by Sopris West Educational Services, and are used by permission of the author.

Who is ready for PGM?

Students should have been exposed to phonological awareness instruction and beginning reading instruction. They should be able to:

1. Give a sound for each consonant letter and digraphs. For example:
   m = / m /; **z** = / z /; **sh** = / sh /

2. Blend up to five phonemes together orally. For example:
   / sh / / ĕ / / l / = **shell**   / t / / w / / ĭ / / s / / t / = **twist**

3. Isolate, pronounce, and change the beginning, middle, and end sounds in a three-phoneme spoken word. For example:
   Change the / m / in *map* to / z / (*zap*)
   Change the / s / in *pass* to / t / (*pat*)
   Change the / ĭ / in *kid* to / ŭ / (*cud*)

4. Orally segment a spoken word with three to four phonemes. For example:
   edge = / ĕ / / j /
   slop = / s / / l / / ŏ / / p /
   shop = / sh / / ŏ / / p /

5. Distinguish among short vowel sounds, with the help of a cue card or key words.

6. Name all letters.

7. Read at least at a mid-first grade level, with 50 to 100 sight words learned.

How much instructional time is recommended for PGM?

The procedure can be used with a whole class or with small groups. The first session of the week should take 30 minutes; two more practice sessions of 20 minutes will be needed on two additional days to provide enough continuity of instruction.

What equipment is necessary for PGM?

- An organized word list reference (e.g., *Greenwood Word Lists* [Minsky, 2003]).

- 6–10 square tiles for each student to manipulate.

- Phoneme-grapheme mapping paper (large-section grid paper). You can use the mapping grid on page 31 as a master for copying.

- Pencils, plain and colored (or highlighter pens).

- A chart or an overhead projector.

- Overhead transparencies of phoneme-grapheme paper and transparent chips for demonstration.

Reading Big Words: Syllabication and Advanced Decoding

PHONEME-GRAPHEME MAPPING GRID

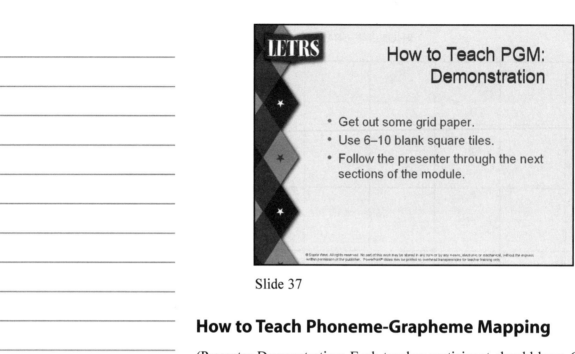

Slide 37

How to Teach Phoneme-Grapheme Mapping

(Presenter Demonstration: Each teacher participant should have 6–10 blank square tiles and several sheets of PGM grid paper. The leader should model this process, using grid paper on an overhead transparency.)

1. Introduce the new concept; model and explain the sound or sound pattern of the lesson.[3]

    Example: "Say *sing*. What's the last sound you feel as you say that word? Yes, it's / ng /. This sound goes through your nose while your tongue comes up and touches the back of your throat. No English word begins with / ng /."

2. Using an overhead projector, point to a row of boxes on the grid. Tell students they will segment words or syllables into phonemes by moving one tile for each speech sound.

    Say: "One square tile equals one sound, not one letter. We'll say the word, then say each phoneme while we move a tile."

    Example: "Watch me. *Sing.* / s / / ĭ / / ng /." (Move each tile into a box—a total of three boxes—as you say each phoneme.)

    "Let's do another one together. *Long.* / l / / ŏ / / ng /." (Students say each sound and move their tiles with the leader demonstrating on the overhead.)

    "What's the word? What does the last tile stand for? The second tile?"

    Repeat this step with the words *long, bang, wrung, wing.*

32

[3] Note: If students are working on / ng / and **ng**, they already knowing the single-consonant correspondences and digraphs **sh**, **ch**, **th**, **wh**, and **ck**. They know that the plural can sound like / s / or / z /. Blends are segmented; each letter in a blend corresponds to one speech sound.

3. Now show students a list of words that demonstrate the concept you are working on. Have students:

   • Read the word list (below) silently, then out loud together.

   • Identify the target phoneme / ng / and grapheme **ng** in each word.

   • Circle the target grapheme **ng** in each word.

   | *wing* | *throngs* | *wings* | *slung* | *strength* |
   | *wrong* | *stung* | *thongs* | *length* | *slingshot* |

4. Turn attention to the phoneme-grapheme mapping paper.

   • Say: "We are going to see how the sounds (phonemes) in the word map to the letters (graphemes) in the word. Look at the mapping paper. We'll use one box for the letter or letters (graphemes) that correspond to each of the speech sounds (phonemes). You'll always have the same number of boxes as you have sounds in the word."

   • Say the word. Say each sound as you move a tile into a corresponding box.

   • Say the sound the first tile represents. Now, slide the tile above the box and write the grapheme (letter or letters) that spells that sound inside the box.

   • Say the sound the second tile represents. Now, slide the tile above the box and write the grapheme that spells that sound inside the box.

   • Continue with all the sounds. Say: "What do you hear? What do you write?" Read the whole word that was written, blending the sounds left to right, if necessary.

   Examples:

wing / w / / ĭ / / ng /	w	i	ng			
wings / w / / ĭ / / ng / / z /	w	i	ng	s		
throngs / th / / r / / ŏ / / ng / / z /	th	r	o	ng	s	
strength / s / / t / / r / / ĕ / / ng / / th /	s	t	r	e	ng	th

   • Have students summarize the concept in their own words, such as: "A box stands for one speech sound or phoneme. A grapheme spells a phoneme but can be more than one letter. The / ng / sound is spelled with **ng** most of the time."

5. Introduce the words *sink*, *bonk*, *tank*. Count the phonemes in each word, and map the words. Ask students to feel where their tongue is for the sound represented by the letter **n** (the back of the throat). Ask students what sound the **n** stands for before the sound / k / (Answer: / ng /). The phoneme / ng / is spelled with the letter **n** before / k / or / g /, as in *sank*, *bunk*, *ankle*, *language*, *finger*.)

6. Practice reading and writing words with the target sound-spelling pattern and those already learned. Appropriate decodable text should be used as necessary to reinforce recognition of the patterns.

Sequence for Teaching Six Common Syllable Types

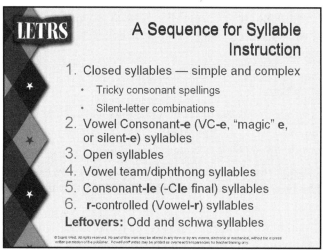

Slide 38

PGM can be used to teach the six basic syllable patterns of English, beginning with closed syllables. Single syllables can be mapped and then combined into multisyllabic words. A spoken syllable is a unit of speech organized around a vowel sound; a written syllable follows conventions for spelling short, long, diphthong, and schwa (unaccented) vowels. Written syllable breaks do not always match the natural breaks in spoken words. Closed syllables with short vowels are "closed off" or "guarded" at the end by one or more consonants; they are the most common type of syllable in the English language.

Each syllable type is presented in the following section. PGM and other activities may be used to acquaint students with these spelling conventions. Closed syllables are usually taught first. Programs vary in the order of syllable instruction; however, there is no one proven approach for teaching this aspect of word structure.

Table 10.3 Six Types of Syllables in English Orthography

Syllable Type	Examples	Definition
1. Closed	*dap* ple *bev* erage	A syllable with a short vowel spelled with one vowel letter ending in one or more consonants.
2. Vowel Consonant-**e** (VC**e**, "magic" **e**, or silent-**e**)	com *pete* des *pite*	A syllable with a long vowel spelled with one vowel + one consonant + silent **e**.
3. Open	*pro* gram *ta* ble *re* cent	A syllable that ends with a long vowel sound, spelled with a single vowel letter.
4. Vowel Team/Diphthong	*awe* some *train* er con *geal* *spoil* age	A syllable with a long or short vowel spelling that uses a vowel combination. Diphthongs **ou** / **ow** and **oi** / **oy** are included in this category.
5. Consonant-**le** (-C**le**)	bi *ble* bea *gle* lit *tle*	An unaccented final syllable containing a consonant before / l /, followed by a silent **e**.
6. **r**-controlled (Vowel-**r**)	*spur* ious con *sort* *char* ter	A syllable with **er**, **ir**, **or**, **ur**, **ar**. Vowel pronunciation is affected by the / r / that follows it.
Leftovers: Odd and schwa	gar *b<u>a</u>ge* act *<u>i</u>ve* fur *n<u>i</u> ture*	Often an unaccented final syllable with a "schwa" vowel. Connecting syllables.

Mapping the Sounds and Syllables

1. **Closed Syllables—Simple and Complex**

   a. Simple—no digraphs or blends
   Example Words (single-syllable): *lap, top, cat, nip, ten, bit*

   b. Simple—with digraphs
   Example Words (single-syllable): *wish, much, thing, chock*

   c. Complex—with blends and digraphs
   Example Words (single-syllable): *bump, shrink, splash, twist*

➤Tricky Consonants

   • digraphs **sh**, **th**, **ck**, **wh**, **ch**, **ng**
   Example Words: *shag, thick, which, thing*

   • position spellings **-tch**, **-dge**
   Example Words: *pitch, dodge*

   • consonants **qu**, **x**
   Example Words: *quilt, quit, ax, fox, index, relax*

   • consonant doubles **ff**, **ll**, **ss**, **zz**
   Example Words: *staff, shell, moss, jazz*

   • plural **s** (/ s /, / z /, / ĭz /)
   Example Words: *snaps, skins, boxes*

   • soft **c** and **g**
   Example Words: *dance, bulge, gym, gem, gist, cent, city, cinch, cyst, cell*

➤Silent-Letter Combinations

   • **kn**, **gn**, **gh**, **wr**
   Example Words: *knot, gnat, ghastly, wrap*

A grid is provided on page 37 for mapping practice with these sounds and syllables.

**Mapping Practice With Closed Syllables, Tricky Consonants,
and Silent-Letter Combinations**

Create vowel sound cue cards with keywords and pictures, and post them on a wall or paste them on individual student's desks:

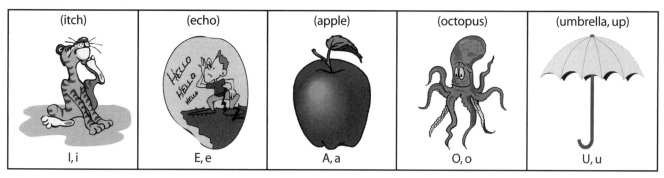

Exercise #3: Mapping Two Closed Syllables

- ♦ Write the words using phoneme-grapheme mapping. Underline each sounded vowel; each creates a syllable.

- ♦ Write the whole word and scoop the syllables after the graphemes are mapped. (The first two words are broken down for you as examples.)

1. unzip	<u>u</u>	n	z	<u>i</u>	p			
2. strongbox	s	t	r	<u>o</u>	ng	b	<u>o</u>	x
3. catnip								
4. public								
5. nutshell								
6. whiplash								
7. quicksand								
8. bankrupt								
9. spendthrift								

1. _unzip_   4. _____   7. _____

2. _strongbox_   5. _____   8. _____

3. _____   6. _____   9. _____

2. **Vowel Consonant-e (VC-e, "magic" e, or silent-e) Syllables**

The silent-**e** syllable has a long vowel sound spelled with one vowel letter, followed by one consonant and a silent **e**. It's also known as the VC-**e** syllable. The silent **e** is "magic" because it can reach back over the single consonant, bonk the vowel, and make it say its own name. The "magic" **e** cannot, however, reach back over two consonants to influence a vowel (e.g., *ridge*, *bronze*, and *mince* are not VC-**e** syllables). A digraph between the vowel and a silent **e** functions as a single consonant because it represents one consonant (*clothe*, *bathe*).

Example words:

> *cute, robe, side, cane*
>
> *fire, inspire, admire; care, glare, square*
>
> *fishline, homemade, campfire, classmate, costume, athlete, clockwise*

f	i	sh	l	i	n	e̶			

3. **Open Syllables**

Open syllables end in long vowel sounds that are spelled with one vowel letter. Except for the few word families with single open syllables—*me, he, she, we; so, go, no;* and *my, try, by, cry*—open syllables combine with others in multisyllabic words. The final syllable **y**, sounding like a long **e**, is an open syllable.

lady

l	a	d	y			

robot

reflex

butane

Exercise #4: Multisyllable Words With Open Syllables

♦ Map these open-syllable words on the grid.

♦ Underline the vowels in the open syllables to distinguish them from the "magic" **e** and closed syllables.

1. female	5. dizzy
2. behave	6. frequent
3. polite	7. relax
4. robot	8. microscope

1.
2.
3.
4.
5.
6.
7.
8.

4. **Vowel Team/Diphthong Syllables**

Vowel teams are graphemes that can represent long vowel sounds, short vowel sounds, or diphthongs (**ou**, **oi**). Vowel teams can be two letters (e.g., **ai**, **ay**, **ei**, **ea**), three letters (e.g., **igh**, **eau**), or four letters (e.g., **eigh**, **ough**, **augh**). That is why the term *vowel team* is preferred to *vowel digraph*, which is not used in LETRS.

Some vowel team spellings are determined by the position of a sound in a syllable.

Table 10.4 Vowel Team Spellings by Position of Vowel Sound

Vowel Sound	Frequently Used Teams		Less Frequently Used Teams
	Beginning/Middle of Word	End of Word	
long **a**	**ai** *rain, rail*	**ay** *ray*	**eigh, ei, ey, ea** *eight, vein, they, break*
long **e**	**ee, ea** *beet, beat*	—	**ie, ei, ey** *piece, ceiling, key*
long **i**	**igh** *sight*	—	**ie** *lie*
long **o**	**oa** *boat*	**ow** *snow*	**ough, ou, oe** *although, shoulder, oboe*
long **u**	**oo, ou** *food, soup*	**ew** *stew*	**ui, ue** *suit, blue*
glided long **u** (/ yū /)			**ue, ew, eu** *cue, few, Europe*
diphthong **ou**	**ou** *ground* **ow + l, n, d** *owl, down, crowd*	**ow** *now*	
diphthong **oi**	**oi** *avoid, boil*	**oy** *boy, toy*	
/ aw /	**au** *laundry* **aw + n, l** *lawn, crawl*	**aw** *saw, claw*	**ough** *(cough)*, **augh** *(caught)*, **all** *(call)*, **al** *(walk)*

Exercise #5: Vowel Team Syllables

◆ Underline all the vowel teams in the following words.

◆ Check to see if the patterns fit with those in Table 10.4.

maintain	subway	crayon	beefsteak
daylight	highway	tightrope	cyclone
between	disappear	relief	squeamish
snowflake	raincoat	poached	poultry
mushroom	coupon	mildew	shampoo
pewter	Europe	barbecue	woodbox
ointment	rejoined	cowboy	enjoyment
cowboy	destroy	avoid	rejoin
playground	astound	proudly	notebook

---

5. **Consonant-le (-Cle) Syllables**

A Consonant-**le** combination at the end of multisyllabic words such as *maple*, *bugle*, *scrabble*, and *nozzle* is a whole syllable unit. Mapping is tricky, because the sounds are Consonant + unaccented vowel (schwa) + / l / in **-ble**, **-gle**, and so forth. The vowel letter **e** is there as a marker, but it does not stand for a vowel sound after the / l / sound. In some words, the unaccented vowel before / l / is barely heard. It would be legitimate to map this last sound with a single letter **l** in one box, because the / l / embodies both the vowel and the consonant. This mapping solution, however, would be confusing to students who have been taught that every syllable must have a vowel.

Consider these words:

A	B
scrabble	maple
gentle	title
puzzle	bugle
pickle	ogle
jostle	ladle

_____

_____

_____

_____

_____

_____

_____

_____

_____

◆ What kind of vowel is in the first syllable of words in column A?

◆ What kind of vowel is in the first syllable of words in column B?

◆ How many consonants are between the vowel and the **-le** in the words in column A?

The juncture of a closed syllable with a **-Cle** syllable produces a sequence of two or more consonants before the **-le** (*trample, skittle*). Thus, the vowel in the first syllable is short; it is closed off, or guarded, by a consonant. If the same letter is doubled, however, only one sound is heard. Sometimes a **t** in **st** is silent, as in *thistle* and *wrestle*. A **ck** represents one sounded / k /, as in *trickle*.

If an open syllable is joined with a **-Cle** syllable—as in *noble, title,* or *bugle*—the vowel sound of the first syllable is free to say its long sound because the single consonant before **-le** belongs to the **-Cle** syllable unit. A vowel team syllable can also be joined with **-Cle**, as in *steeple, noodle,* or *beagle.*

Exercise #6: Identifying **-Cle** Syllables

◆ Separate the final **-Cle** syllable in the following words by scooping under it. Then, isolate the vowel sound of the first syllable.

◆ Identify whether the first syllable is closed (C), open (O), VC-**e**, or a vowel team (VT). (Note that a doubled consonant in spelling corresponds to one *spoken* phoneme.)

_____ frazzle	_____ eagle	_____ fickle
_____ title	_____ maple	_____ droodle
_____ battle	_____ trestle	_____ muscle
_____ ogle	_____ bridle	_____ scruple
_____ little	_____ gentle	_____ scramble
_____ unstable	_____ steeple	_____ inveigle

Reading Big Words: Syllabication and Advanced Decoding

6. r-controlled (Vowel-r) Syllables

A vowel is either welded together with or influenced by an / r / that follows. The / er / combination is one welded sound that cannot be segmented into a vowel and consonant; it is spelled variously as **ir** *(fir)*, **ur** *(burn)*, **er** *(her)*, **or** *(word)*, or **ar** *(backward)*. The first three spelling combinations are the most common. The / or / and / ar / combinations—spelled **or** *(for)* and **ar** *(star)*—are partially welded, or coarticulated. In phoneme-grapheme mapping, put those letters in one sound box. If words follow a VC-**e** pattern—such as *fare*, *pore*, or *ire*—treat them as VC-**e** syllables. If vowel teams are used for the sounds, treat them as vowel team syllables *(steer, fair, pour)*.

Map these words on the grid:

/ er /	/ ar /	/ or /
stir	star	for
turn	bar	nor
letter	barnyard	forlorn

l	e	tt	er					

Vowel-**r** sounds have multiple spellings. They must be taught gradually—in steps—and retaught as word families and patterns. Examples of other spelling patterns are:

/ er /	/ ar /	/ or /
dollar, exemplar professor, proctor	heart bizarre	pour floor store

Other patterns:

  marry, carry
  merit, very, terrible, merry, error

Other principles for reading and spelling words with Vowel-**r** combinations:

◆ When the letters **ar** are unaccented at the end a word, they sound like / er /:

  dollar, polar, perpendicular

◆ When the letters **or** are unaccented at the end of a word, they sound like / er /:

  proctor, confessor, stressor

◆ When the letters **ar** and **or** follow the letter **w**, their sounds are changed:

  thwart, war, ward, award, wart

  worthy, worth, word, worm, worst, worry

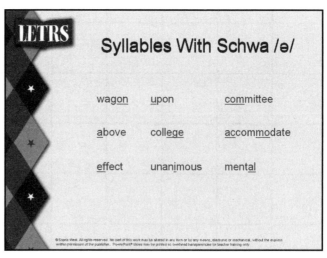

Slide 39

Leftovers: Odd and Schwa (/ə/) Syllables

When syllables are combined in longer words, one receives primary stress or accent. The other syllable(s) may then be unstressed or unaccented, leaving the vowel sound pronounced in an indistinct manner. Most odd syllables are unaccented and contain a schwa sound. A vowel that has been emptied of its distinguishing features is called *schwa*, a Yiddish word for "empty."

Here are some examples:

cement   garb<u>age</u>   def<u>i</u>nition   c<u>o</u>mmit

capt<u>ai</u>n   furn<u>i</u>ture   wag<u>o</u>n   bag<u>e</u>l

Students can handle this concept. Tell them what's at work; don't tell them they are saying the word the wrong way when they make a schwa sound.

Review of Syllable Types: Sort and Combine

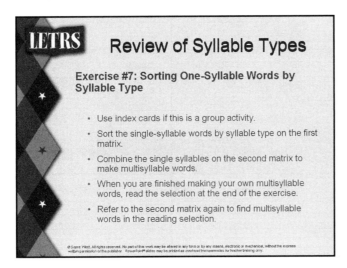

Slide 40

Exercise #7: Sorting One-Syllable Words by Syllable Type

♦ Working with a partner, use the grid below to sort these one-syllable words by syllable type.

wait	with	spire	views	rod	large
height	means	when	by	first	he
kite	took	length	take	walk	fields

Closed	-C**le**	Open

Vowel Team	Vowel-**r**	VC-**e** ("magic" **e**)

Exercise #7 *(continued)*

♦ The syllables below are sorted into the chart categories. Combine any number of syllables to make words. (If this is done in a group, each person can take a syllable card—or two— and then find the person with a match that makes a word.)

♦ In the next reading selection, you can find words to make with these syllables:

pub	meth	con	same	e-	doc	mat	light	point
an-	pur	oc-	com	bet	ac-	re-	thun	pre-
prop	ex-	op-	ap-	storm	un-	lish	od	cern
-ness	lect	tor	ter	-ing	-ed	swer	pose	cur
mon	ter	cess	gions	-der	pare	-er	tend	por
tune	suc	-ful	proach					

Closed	-C**le**	Open
pub, meth, con, doc, mat, an-, oc-, com, bet, ac-, thun, prop, ex-, op-, ap-, un-, lish, od, -ness, lect, -ing, -ed, mon, cess, tend, suc, -ful	(none)	e-, re-, pre-

Vowel Team	Vowel-**r**	VC-e ("magic" **e**)
light, point, gions, proach	pur, storm, cern, tor, ter, swer, cur, ter, -der, -er, por	same, pose, pare, tune

Words created by combining syllables:

_____   _____

_____   _____

_____   _____

_____   _____

_____   _____

Exercise #7 *(continued)*

This famous excerpt from Ben Franklin's diaries,[4] in which he describes his experiment with flying a kite during a lightning storm to prove that electricity could be harnessed, contains words with the combined syllables.

…The Doctor, having published his method of verifying his hypothesis concerning the sameness of electricity with the matter lightning, was waiting for the erection of a spire in Philadelphia to carry his views into execution, not imagining that a pointed rod of a moderate height could answer the purpose, when it occurred to him that by means of a common kite he could have better access to the regions of thunder than by any spire whatever. Preparing, therefore, a large silk handkerchief and two cross-sticks of a proper length on which to extend it, he took the opportunity of the first approaching thunderstorm to take a walk in the fields, in which there was a shed convenient for his purpose. But, dreading the ridicule which too commonly attends unsuccessful attempts in science, he communicated his intended experiment to nobody but his son who assisted him in raising the kite.

—Written by Joseph Priestley with Ben Franklin's guidance in 1767

[4] Lemisch, L.J. (Ed.) (1999). *Benjamin Franklin: The autobiography and other writings* (pp. 232–233). New York: Signet Classics.

Special Final Syllables

Odd Syllables Out

garb<u>age</u>   furn<u>iture</u>   ac<u>tive</u>

na<u>tion</u>   spe<u>cial</u>   cap<u>tain</u>

con<u>science</u>   mi<u>ssion</u>   par<u>tial</u>

Slide 41

Examine the chart below. The final syllables begin with the speech sound / ch /, / sh /, or / zh /. They are made by combining the letters **ti**, **si**, **sci**, or **ci** with various endings.

	al	ence, ency	on	an	ent	a	ous
ti	partial celestial potential _____ _____	patience _____ _____	nation _____ _____	martian _____ _____	patient _____ _____	militia _____ _____	fictitious _____ _____
si, sci		conscience _____ _____	mission suspension _____	artesian _____ _____	prescient _____ _____	Asia _____ _____	luscious _____ _____
ci	special financial _____ _____	efficiency _____ _____	suspicion _____ _____	musician _____ _____	ancient _____ _____	Marcia _____ _____	vicious _____ _____

Can you think of any more words that have final syllables that begin with **ti**, **si**, **sci**, or **ci** and the endings in the matrix? Add one or two to each box.

Obsolete English Words for Decoding Practice[5]

Word	Meaning
almner	"one who gives and receives alms for the king"
arfname	"an heir"
beblubbered	"swollen"
blutterbunged	"confounded; pixilated"
brizzle	"to scorch near-burning"
bumwhush	"ruin; obscurity"
buzznack	"old organ playing badly"
dwizzen	"to shrink or dry up"
flattybouch	"one who goes from place to place during the summer"
knotchelled	"when a man says he won't pay his wife's debts"
ramfeezled	"to exhaust oneself with work"
skewboglish	"said of a shying horse"
swallocking	"very sultry"
ugsumness	"terribleness"

[5] From Kacirk, J. (2000). *The word museum: The most remarkable English words ever forgotten.* New York: Touchstone Books.

Dividing Words Into Syllables for Decoding Fluency

Knowing phoneme-grapheme correspondences and having an eye for, and an understanding of, syllable conventions in spelling is the first step toward reading big words fluently. Awareness of these chunks also helps students remember how to spell big words. However, additional word decoding strategies are needed. The human eye, or rather, the brain's orthographic processor, must learn to see patterns of letters and recurring word parts.

Most Useful Syllable Division Principles

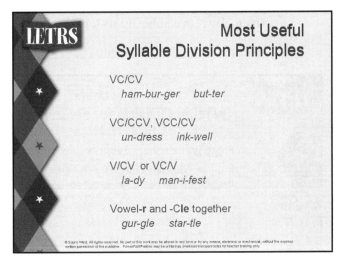

Slide 42

If students develop an eye for common letter sequences through brief, daily practice exercises, they will read words in text more fluently and accurately. Knowing what a word means will help students come up with its pronunciation after the sounds and syllables are decoded.

VC/CV	If two consonants come between two vowels, divide between the consonants. The first vowel will be short.
	din/ner in/vit/ed
VC/CCV	Keep blends and digraphs together when dividing syllables.
	mor/pheme ath/lete a/bridged
VCC/CV	Vowels will almost always be short if the syllable ends in one or more consonants. Divide between words in a compound.
	grand/moth/er long/hand camp/ground

V/CV (75%)
VC/V (25%)

When a single consonant comes between two vowels, three-quarters of the time the first syllable will be open and the vowel will be long, so divide after the vowel and give it its long sound. If that does not make a recognized word, try the other option, which works one-quarter of the time. Group the consonant with the vowel, close off the first syllable, and give the vowel its short sound.

fa/vor/ite	e/nough
scav/en/ger	hal/i/but

-Cle

Keep a Consonant-**le** together at the end of a word.

cy/cle	ta/ble

Vowel-r

Keep Vowel-**r** combinations together.

wor/thy	fa/vor/ite

LETRS

Syllable Division for Reading

• Read the "Salmon Summer" excerpt.

• Find words with two or more syllables that might be used for word study. Underline them.

Slide 43

Exercise #8: Applying Syllable Division Principles

◆ Read this fourth grade passage about an Aleut boy who lives in Alaska and is learning to fish with his family.[6]

◆ Underline the words with two or more syllables that might be used for word study.

◆ After studying the syllable division rules above, find several examples of words that could be used to demonstrate each rule. Write the words in the correct column of the grid, which appears after the passage.

…Alex loves to snack on tamuuq (tah-MOHK), chewy, dry fish. This tamuuq comes from halibut, his favorite fish to catch. But now that the salmon are running, Alex is going fishing for salmon.

He's been waiting for them to return. As young fry, they left the nearby stream to live at sea. To complete their life cycle, they're coming back to the same stream to spawn.

This summer, nine-year-old Alex is finally old enough to help his father set the gill net. Like their Aleut (AL-ee-oot) ancestors, they catch fish to feed their family.

By next morning, the net is full of flapping fish. They are trapped in the almost-invisible mesh of the net as they try to swim past Alex's beach. Alex and his father pull their net. It's time to "pick" fish.

Alex wears gloves to protect his hands not only from the fine mesh of the nets but also from the stings of jellyfish. It's not as much fun as fishing with a line, but there will be time for that later. Now they must finish landing today's catch.

…Alex cleans salmon alongside his father as seagulls watch from afar. He uses the same knife his grandmother's uncle used to skin bears. He cuts filets from one of the fish for dinner. With the others, he cuts off the head, pulls out the guts, and leaves the skin and tails on. They're for the smokehouse. But as the cleaned fish hang outside, uninvited visitors fly in to steal a meal.

…Alex leaves salmon scraps to wash away with the tide and be eaten by scavengers. The gulls swoop down for a fish feast. As always, they eat their favorite part of the salmon first—the eyes.

[6] McMillan, B. (1996). Salmon summer. In *Traditions*, Houghton Mifflin Reading: The Nation's Choice© Edition (pp. 635–640). Boston: Houghton Mifflin School. Used by permission.

Exercise #8 *(continued)*

VC/CV	VC/CCV VCC/CV	V/CV VC/V	-Cle
_____	_____	_____	_____
_____	_____	_____	_____
_____	_____	_____	_____
_____	_____	_____	_____
_____	_____	_____	_____
_____	_____	_____	_____
_____	_____	_____	_____
_____	_____	_____	_____
_____	_____	_____	_____
_____	_____	_____	_____

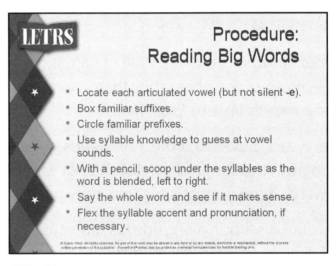

Slide 44

Basic Procedure for Reading Big Words[7]

1. Locate and put a line under each vowel grapheme in the word (but not final silent-**e**'s). Vowel teams are one vowel sound.

2. Box any familiar endings, such as **-ing**, **-ed**, or **-ful**.

3. Circle any familiar beginning word parts, such as **re-**, **un-**, or **mis-**.

4. Use knowledge of syllables to decode the vowel sounds.

[7] Archer et al. *Rewards* program teaches students to read words using similar strategies.

5. With a pencil, scoop under each syllable, blending the sounds left to right.

6. Say the whole word and see if it makes sense. Flex the syllable accent; try saying the word different ways if it doesn't sound right.

7. Check the context for clarification. Ask if you don't know the word.

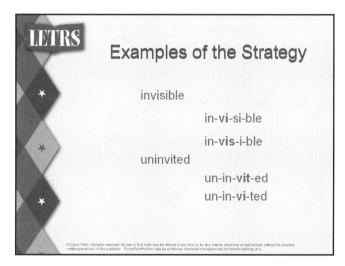

Slide 45

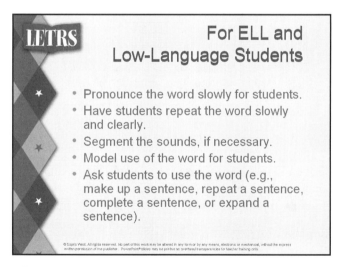

Slide 46

Syllabication for Spelling[8]

Use magnetized syllable blocks with an erasable surface that can be stuck to a magnetized white board.

in	vis	i	ble

---

[8] This practice was learned from Linda Farrell, National LETRS trainer and director of Reading Street.

Say a word to students (e.g., *invisible*).

1. Students repeat the word.

2. Students place a blank syllable block for each spoken syllable.

3. Teacher pronounces each syllable while students write the letters on each syllable block.

4. Teacher helps students segment the sounds and remember spelling correspondences and patterns, giving clues as necessary.

5. Students write the whole word as a unit and read it back.

6. Students cover up the prompt and write the word from memory.

Sight Recognition and Irregular Words

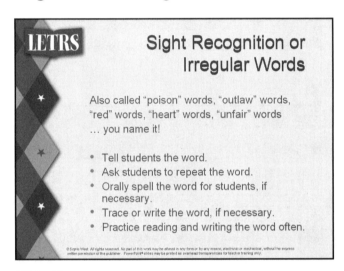

Slide 47

In proficient reading, we recognize most words "by sight"—that is, without having to analyze them. Sight recognition is generally a result of lots of practice seeing words in print. Reading "by sight" is not limited to irregular words.

Some words, however, are irregular; they don't follow patterns. Irregular words tend to be from Anglo-Saxon, and they comprise the oldest, most common words in the English language. They must be identified and approached differently in instruction. This simple procedure works most of the time:

• Tell students the word.

• Ask students, "What word?"

• Read the word again with students.

If students need more practice, have them say the letters out loud while tracing over them or writing them on a rough surface such as fiberboard or a carpet square, or a cookie tray with pudding or sand in it. Then ask them to say the whole word and read it in a phrase or sentence.

Exercise #9: Scooping Under Syllables

♦ Remember this gem? Mark the syllable divisions in the multisyllable words.

♦ Then, practice scooping the syllables with your pencil as you read the words.

To stabilize the pretractal fordex, the brave engineer resituated the gyrine. Then he tribled the cabulum.

"Oh, whippers!" he exclaimed. "Thank heavens, I'm no longer befuddled by this problem."

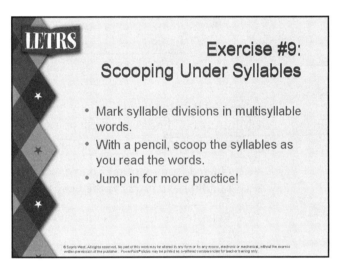

Slide 48

♦ Here's more practice if you need it! Scoop the syllable divisions in the italicized words, using syllable division principles. Show another person how to read those words.

Snow *blindness* is a *temporary* loss of sight caused by bright sunlight *reflected* from snow. It usually lasts from *several* days to a week. *Occasionally*, the person will have trouble *distinguishing* between colors after snow blindness and sees everything colored red for a time. In most cases, snow blindness *disappears* when a person rests the eyes and remains indoors. Wearing *sunglasses* or *goggles* usually *prevents* snow blindness.[9]

[9] Williams, J. (1992). *The weather book* (p. 105). New York: Vintage Books.

Don't Forget To Build Fluency

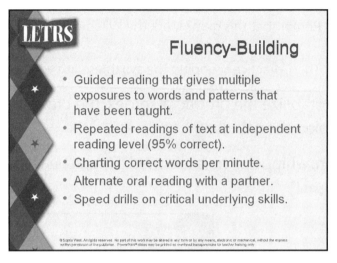

Slide 49

Another LETRS module extensively explores the issue of reading fluency. In brief, fluency-building is an aspect of every well-taught reading lesson. It can be accomplished in these ways:

1. Guided reading of decodable text or other controlled text that gives multiple exposures to the words and patterns that have been taught.

2. Repeated readings of text that can be read at a 95% accuracy level.

3. Charting increments of gain in timed, repeated readings.

4. Alternate oral reading with a peer or adult model.

5. Speed drills on critical underlying skills.

Morphology: Meaningful Word Parts

The Morphological Layer of Language for Reading, Spelling, and Vocabulary

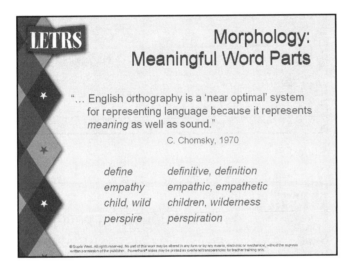

Slide 50

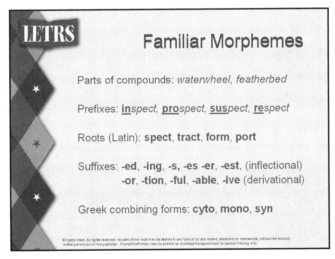

Slide 51

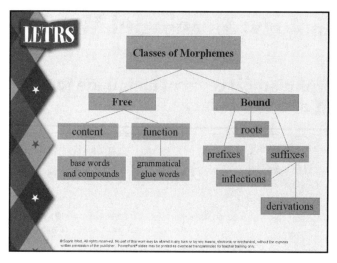

Slide 52

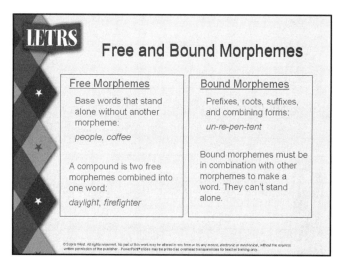

Slide 53

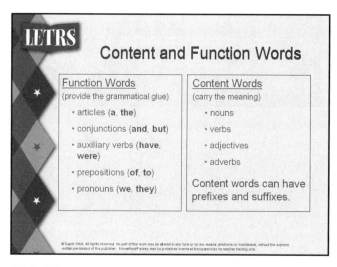

Slide 54

Morphemes are the smallest meaningful units in language; they may be one syllable or many. Words are made up of one or more morphemes. Morphemes may be **free** or **bound**. If a morpheme is free, it can stand alone as a word. If a morpheme is bound, it can be found only in combination with other morphemes. Free morphemes include base words and the parts of compounds made from those base words. Bound morphemes include grammatical endings; prefixes, roots, and suffixes from the Latin layer of English; and Greek combining forms, such as **poly** and **chrome**.

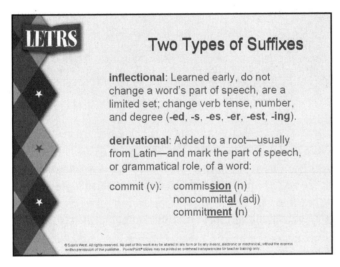

Slide 55

Suffix morphemes are of two types: **inflectional** and **derivational**. Anglo-Saxon words use consistent spellings for **inflections** (grammatical endings), including the past tense **-ed**, the plurals **-s** and **-es**, the comparatives **-er** and **-est**, the present tense marker **-s**, and the **-ing** added to gerunds and present tense verbs (she *walks*; *walking* is not strenuous; I am *walking* ahead). Inflections do not change the part of speech of the word to which they are added.

Inflectional suffixes are known by children in oral language before they come to school. Inflections are tough to avoid in beginning reading and spelling instruction, so they should be addressed beginning in first grade. These are examples of inflections:

Matilda rais<u>ed</u> the pig from its infancy.

The pig was larg<u>er</u> than her favorite dog.

The pig was the smart<u>est</u> animal in the household.

Liv<u>ing</u> with the pig, however, provid<u>ed</u> certain challenges.

Plural Inflectional Suffix

/ s /	/ z /	/ ĭz /
sheets	dogs	horses
picnics	hens	hitches
turnips	doves	axes
puffs	birds	bridges
baths	cows	cheeses

Slide 56

The plural in English is pronounced variously as / s / (as in *ropes*), / z / (as in *drums*), and / ĭz / (as in *peaches*). Only the / ĭz / form makes a syllable. The syllable / ĭz / is added after selected fricatives and affricates (e.g., *sexes*, *passes*, *peaches*, *wishes*, *mixes*, *garages*). Children tend to spell the plural phonetically until they consolidate their morphological skill (e.g., FREDZ [*friends*] and BEHEZ [*beaches*]).

Irregular plural and past tense forms such as sheep, children, went, and forgot are difficult for many children and must be taught and practiced for speaking, reading, and writing. Children must learn that regular inflectional morphemes—such as the past tense **-ed**—have stable spellings even though their pronunciation varies.

Past Tense Inflectional Suffix

/ t /	/ d /	/ ĭd /
matched	preferred	invented
blessed	hummed	slotted
picked	raved	offended
stepped	vowed	boarded
coughed	spoiled	chided

Slide 57

Exercise #10: Hearing and Mapping Three Sounds of Past Tense **-ed**

English spelling is "deep" or "morphophonological." That means that spelling shows meaningful parts of words even if those spellings do not correspond directly to sound. The first example of this principle is the **-ed** ending.

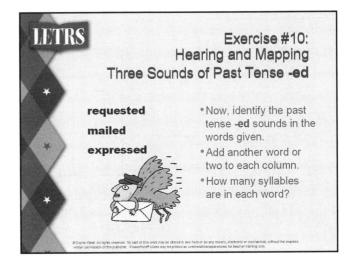

LETRS

Exercise #10:
Hearing and Mapping
Three Sounds of Past Tense -ed

requested

mailed

expressed

• Now, identify the past tense **-ed** sounds in the words given.
• Add another word or two to each column.
• How many syllables are in each word?

◆ Sort these words in the grid columns by their last sound.

Slide 58

rushed	filled	ended	crossed
invented	asked	dusted	smiled
blazed	wilted	mined	jumped

/ t /	/ d /	/ ĭd /

◆ Add another word or two of your own to each column.

◆ How many syllables are in each word? (Some have more morphemes than they have syllables.) In many past tense words, the morpheme is just a phoneme—not a syllable—as in *begged, formed, spilled,* and *passed.*

How would you map these words?

yelled   knocked   twisted

In the beginning stages of spelling, children attend to the sounds in words before they attend to the meaningful parts, so they write TAKT for *talked*, JRAGD for *dragged*, and WATID for *waited*. They need systematic practice to internalize the relationship between sound, spelling, and meaning.

Advanced Concept!

When past tense **-ed** is added to a base word that ends in a voiced consonant, the ending is pronounced / d /. When past tense **-ed** is added to a base word that ends in a voiceless consonant, the ending is pronounced / t /. (When the **-ed** is pronounced as just one consonant sound, it is placed in just one box for phoneme-grapheme mapping.) Exceptions are base words that end in / t / or / d / (*rant, mend*), as they add a whole / ĭd / syllable.

Spelling Rules for Adding Endings

Slide 59

There are three major spelling rules that operate when endings are added to words. They are important for both reading and spelling. The rules are much easier to learn and teach if syllable constructions are already understood.

1a. Consonant Doubling.

When a one-syllable word with one vowel ends in one consonant, double the final consonant before adding a suffix beginning with a vowel (*wettest*, *sinner*, *crabbing*). Do not double the consonant if the suffix begins with a consonant (<u>shipment</u>, <u>winless</u>)

1b. Advanced Consonant Doubling.

When a word has more than one syllable—and if the final syllable is accented and has one vowel followed by one consonant—double the final consonant when adding an ending beginning with a vowel (*referred* vs. *collared*; *imbedded* vs. *signaling*).

2. Drop the silent-e.

When a root word ends in a silent-**e**, drop the **e** when adding a suffix beginning with a vowel (e.g., *blame*: *blaming*; *paste*: *pasted*). Keep the **e** before a suffix beginning with a consonant (e.g., *confine*: *confinement*; *extreme*: *extremely*).

3. Change Y to I.

When a root ends in a **y** preceded by a consonant, change **y** to **i** before a suffix, except **-ing**. If the root word ends in a **y** preceded by a vowel (e.g., **ay**, **ey**, **uy**, **oy**), just add the suffix. (Note that **y** changes to **i** even if the suffix begins with a consonant.)

Exercise #11: Which Ending Rule?

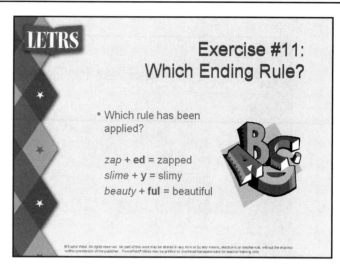

Slide 60

◆ Indicate in the third column of this grid the number of the spelling rule that was applied to the new ending of the base word.

Base	Word With Ending	Rule Number
study	studious	3
grime	grimy	
happen	happened	
refer	referral	
enjoy	enjoyment	
peace	peacefully	

Discovering Assimilated or Chameleon Prefixes

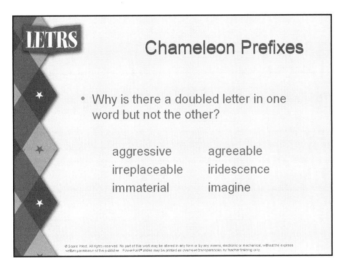

Slide 61

Slide 62

When longer, Latin-derived words are spelled with a doubled consonant letter between the first and second syllables, that doubled letter often indicates that a prefix and a root have been joined. But sometimes, you need to look a little closer. Consider the word *suffix*. Only one phoneme is pronounced at the syllable juncture, so the pronunciation does not give the prefix's identity away. However, the spelling of the word does. The doubled letter results when the last sound-spelling in the prefix—in this case, the *sub* in *suffix*—is changed to match the first sound of the root.

A few prefixes, as listed in the chart below, are very changeable; they adapt to the root to which they are added, but the doubled letter in the word gives them away.

ad- ("to, toward")	**com-** ("with")	**dis-** ("not")	**in-** ("not")	**sub-** ("under")
assimilate	correlate	dissatisfied	innocent	subversion
appeal	connected	differentiate	immaterial	surrogate
addiction	collection		irreligious	suppress
affection			illegal	suffocate
attract				suffix

Can you think of more words that follow these patterns?

_____

_____

_____

_____

_____

_____

_____

_____

_____

_____

_____

_____

_____

_____

_____

_____

_____

_____

_____

_____

_____

Derivational Suffixes, Part of Speech, and Word Pronunciation

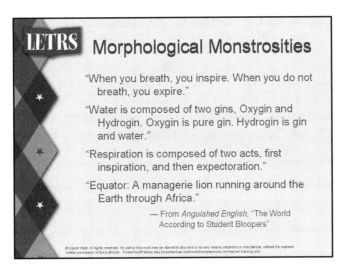

Slide 63

Latin-based **prefixes**, **roots**, and **derivational suffixes** are found in more than 60% of the content words in textbooks. Content words are nouns, verbs, adjectives, and adverbs that determine the unique meaning of the passage. Prefixes, roots, and derivational suffixes are often spelled consistently even though their pronunciation changes within their word family. Consider words such as these:

prevent, prevention, unpreventable

press, pressure, compress, impressive, suppression

mechanic, mechanistic, mechanical

annual, annuity, biannual, semiannually

Slide 64

A **derivational suffix** has a stable spelling and pronunciation, and it includes common endings such as **-ness**, **-less**, **-ful**, **-ous**, **-al**, **-ment**, **-tion**, **-able**, **-ance**, **-ary**, and **-ity**. Importantly, the addition of a derivational suffix changes or determines the grammatical role of the word, or its part of speech. Suffixes such as **-ness**, **-ment**, **-ity**, **-ance**, and **-tion** turn words into nouns; **-less**, **-ful**, **-ous**, **-able**, **-ary**, and **-al** turn words into adjectives; **-ly** turns words into adverbs.

As students become better readers and tackle more challenging words, they will learn the accent or stress patterns in those words. Learning correct pronunciation may be a special challenge for ELL students and those with a "tin ear" for English. Stress patterns in related words often change according to the type of suffix that is added.

Exercise #12: Suffixes and Syllable Stress

♦ Read these word groups and then put an accent mark over the stressed syllable in each word. (As an example, the first word's stressed syllable letter is bold and underlined.)

♦ Note how the vowel sounds have changed in the different forms of each word.

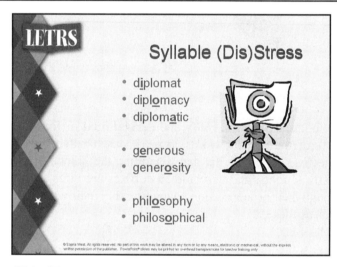

Slide 65

1. phil**o**sophy	2. diplomat	3. nation	4. family
philosopher	diplomacy	national	familial
philosophical	diplomatic	nationality	familiar

Slide 66

Such regular patterns of stress placement and vowel pronunciation are governed by the suffix that is added to a root. When we read, our eyes take in the letters to the right of the fixation point on the root of the word, and our brain very quickly processes the suffix as a known linguistic unit. The phonological processor knows that the suffix requires a certain stress pattern and can then assign a pronunciation to the whole word. To do this, however, the phonological processor must be educated through many exposures to words that follow the patterns created by suffixes. Readers with good vocabularies can pronounce new words by analogy to word patterns they know.

Exercise #13: Syllables and Morphemes

- ◆ Divide each of these words into its morphemes, or meaningful parts. (How to identify a morpheme: 1. You can recognize its meaning; 2. You know other words that use the same morpheme; 3. A dictionary identifies it as one.)

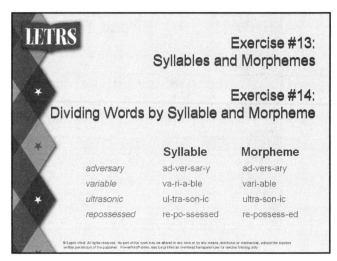

Slide 67

- ◆ Then, count the number of syllables in the word. (The first two words are broken down as examples.)

Word	Morphemes	Number of Word Syllables
prepare	pre-pare	2
phonograph	phono-graph	3
transferable		
adversity		
disspell		
squirmed		
irresistible		
pears		
deceived		
bioluminescence		

Should We Teach Division of Words by Syllable or Morpheme?

Syllable recognition and syllable division are a means to a better end—recognition of morphemes when they are present in a word. We want students to process longer words quickly and accurately and, if possible, quickly process the meanings of the words. Syllable division principles conflict with morpheme division in many words; neither is the "right" or "superior" method. Each represents a different level of word analysis. Whichever way you choose to divide a word, be clear about what level of language organization you want students to attend to.

Exercise #14: Dividing Words by Syllable and Morpheme

♦ Divide these words by syllable and morpheme.

Word	Syllable Division	Morpheme Division
tractor		
poetry		
unicycle		
gentle		
underplayed		

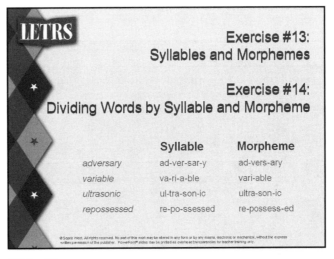

Slide 67

Exercise #15: What Part of Speech?

Derivational suffixes indicate a word's grammatical role or part of speech.

◆ For each word below, indicate whether the word is a noun (**n**), verb (**v**), adjective (**adj**), or adverb (**adv**).

◆ Then, write one more word with another root that has that same suffix.

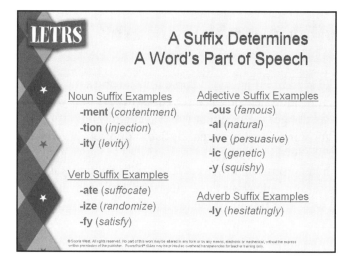

Slide 68

Word	Part of Speech?	Your Word
national	**adj**	impartial, vertical
nationalist		
nationalistically		
nationality		
nationalize		
nationalization		
nationally		
nationhood		
nationless		

Exercise #16: Morphological Word Family Maps

◆ Pick a Latin root from the list on the next page. With a partner or team, create a list of as many words as you can with that root. (A list of common suffixes follows the Latin root list.)

◆ Then, use a transparency or a chart to arrange those words visually to show their relationship to the root. You will create something that looks like a word family tree or web.

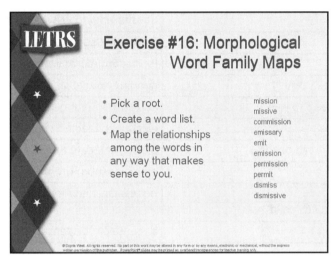

Slide 69

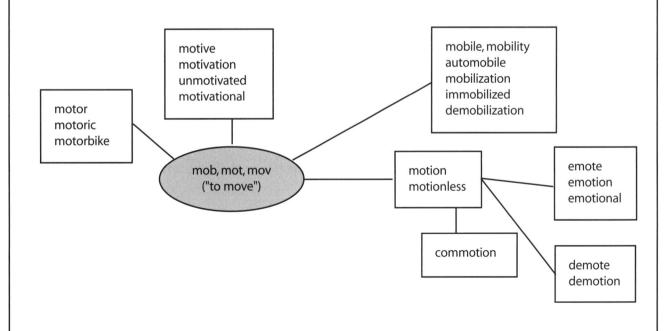

Latin Root	Examples of Words With the Root
cap, cep, cept, ceive, ceit, cip ("to take, catch seize, hold, or receive")	accept, captive, conceive, except, forceps, participate, reception
cede, ceed, cess ("to go, yield, surrender")	secede, recess, necessary, precedent, accessory
cred ("to believe")	credence, credible, credo, credit, incredulous
dict, dic ("to say or to tell")	dictate, addiction, predicament, edict
fac, fact, fect, fic ("to make or do")	fiction, difficult, satisfaction, perfect, infection
fer ("to bear, carry, or yield")	transfer, refer, interfere, aquifer, deferred
flu, fluc, fluv, flux ("to flow")	fluid, influx, confluence, superfluous, fluvial
form ("shape")	formation, informal, perform, conforming
gen, genus ("race, kind, species"; "birth")	genuine, congenial, genetics, homogeneous, gene
grad, gress, gred ("step, degree"; "to walk")	egress, graduate, gradation, digression
jac, ject, jec ("to throw or lie")	ejection, subjected, conjecture, projector
lect, leg, lig ("to choose, pick"; "read or speak")	dialect, delegate, neglect, select, lecture
mit, miss ("to send")	emissary, submit, remittance, permission, dismiss
ped, pod ("foot") (NOT the Greek root **ped** meaning "child")	pedestrian, pedal, podiatrist, podium, pedestal
pend, pens ("to hand or weigh")	dependable, dispensation, appendix, suspend
pos, pon ("to place or set")	suppose, opponent, deposit, poster, position
port ("to carry")	portable, portage, transport, opportunity, import
scrib, script ("to write")	scribe, scripture, description, proscribe
spec, spect, spic ("to see, watch, observe")	inspection, speculate, perspicacious, suspicious, spectral
sta, stit, sist, stet ("to stand")	statue, statute, unstable, distance, establish
tend, tens, tent ("to stretch or strain")	contend, intense, pretension, tenuous, attend
ven, veni, vent ("to come")	venue, intervene, event, adventure, invent
vent ("outlet, opening")	ventilate, vent, vented
vert, vers ("to turn")	university, versatile, versus, vertigo, invert
vid, vis ("to see")	visual, visible, televise, visor, advise
voc, vok ("to call")	vocal, invoke, vocabulary, advocate, voice

Some Common Suffixes:

Noun:	**-ness, -ist, -ism, -or, -er, -tion, -sion, -ment, -ance, -ence, -age, -ture, -ity**
Verb:	**-ate, -ize, -ify**
Adjective:	**-less, -ic, -ish, -y, -ful, -al, -ive, -ent, -ous, -able/-ible, -ary**
Adverb:	**-ly**

Which Words Are Most Difficult to Read and Spell?

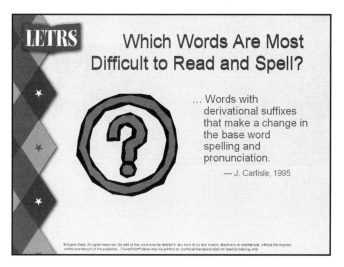

Slide 70

Words with derivational suffixes are not equally easy to remember and use (Carlisle, 1995). Some are straightforward: the ending does not change the base word to which it is added. Some involve a spelling change in the base word but no corresponding change in pronunciation of the base word, and some require a phonological change in the base word. In the chart below, notice how the base word is changed by the suffix added to it.

No Spelling Change in Base Word	Spelling Change in Base Word	Phonological Change in Base Word	Both Spelling and Phonological Changes in Base Word
conformity	sensible	resignation	sanity
enjoyment	happiest	autumnal	sublimation
reportable	occurrence	bombardier	finality
intactness	rebellion	electricity	injurious
		victorious	studious
			definitive

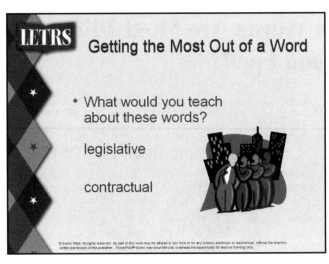

Slide 71

Reading Big Words: Syllabication and Advanced Decoding

Exercise #17: Teaching Decoding of Key Vocabulary

◆ Read this excerpt from *Little Women*.[10]

◆ Select 8–10 multisyllabic words. What features of those words would you want a student to notice, explain, or generalize? Plan one minute of instruction around one or more of the words.

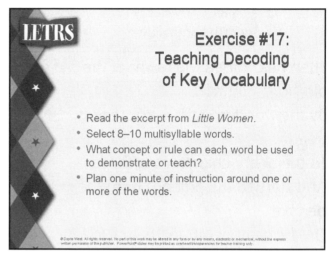

Slide 72

… Fifteen-year-old Jo was very tall, thin, and brown, and reminded one of a colt, for she never seemed to know what to do with her long limbs, which were very much in her way. She had a decided mouth, a comical nose, and sharp, gray eyes, which appeared to see everything, and were by turns fierce, funny, or thoughtful. Her long, thick hair was her one beauty, but it was usually bundled into a net, to be out of her way. Round shoulders had Jo, big hands and feet, a flyaway look to her clothes, and the uncomfortable appearance of a girl who was rapidly shooting up into a woman, and didn't like it.

Selected words:

_____

_____

_____

_____

_____

[10] Alcott, L.M. (originally published in 1868). (2000). *Little women* (pp. 6–7). New York: Scholastic Classics.

Exercise #18: Teaching Assorted Concepts

♦ Read this excerpt from "Paul Revere's Ride," by Henry Wadsworth Longfellow:

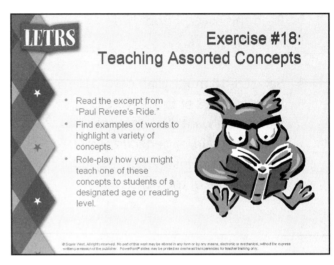

Slide 73

Then he climbed the tower of the old North Church,
By the wooden stairs, with stealthy tread,
To the belfry-chamber overhead,
And startled the pigeons from their perch
On the somber rafters, that round him made
Masses and moving shapes of shade,
By the trembling ladder, steep and tall,
To the highest window in the wall,
Where he paused to listen and look down
A moment on the roofs of the town,
And the moonlight flowing over all.

Beneath, in the churchyard, lay the dead,
In their night-encampment on the hill,
Wrapped in the silence so deep and still
That he could hear, like a sentinel's tread,
The watchful night-wind, as it went
Creeping along from tent to tent,
And seeming to whisper, "All is well!"

...
Meanwhile, impatient to mount and ride,
Booted and spurred, with a heavy stride
On the opposite shore walked Paul Revere.
Now he patted his horse's side,
Now gazed at the landscape far and near

Exercise #18 *(continued)*

Then, impetuous, stamped the earth,
And turned and tightened his saddle-girth;
But mostly he watched with eager search
The belfry tower of the Old North Church,
As it rose above the graves on the hill,
Lonely and spectral and somber and still.
And lo! As he looks, on the belfry's height
A glimmer, and then a gleam of light!
He springs to the saddle, the bridle he turns,
But lingers and gazes, till full on his sight
A second lamp in the belfry burns!"

◆ Find examples of words in the poem you could use to teach the following concepts:
  • Different sounds of the past tense **-ed** (/ t /, / d /, / ĭ d /).

  • Words with Latin roots, prefixes, and suffixes.

  • An assimilated or "chameleon" prefix.

  • Syllable combinations with a Consonant-**le** syllable at the end of the word.

  • Different sounds and spellings for plural endings.

  • Syllable juncture and syllable division patterns.

  • Ending addition rules (e.g., consonant doubling, drop silent-**e**, change **y** to **i**).

◆ If possible, role-play how you might teach **one** of these concepts to students of a designated age or reading level. Follow these steps:
  1. Assemble examples of the concept you wish to teach.

  2. Zero in on the concept and clearly define it.

  3. Plan a presentation of the concept with examples and counter-examples, if necessary.

  4. Demonstrate what you want the students to know or do.

  5. Guide or lead students in successful practice.

  6. Apply in an independent activity.

  7. Give corrective feedback, if necessary, and reteach the concept, if necessary.

Teaching the Reading of Big Words

Principles of Instruction

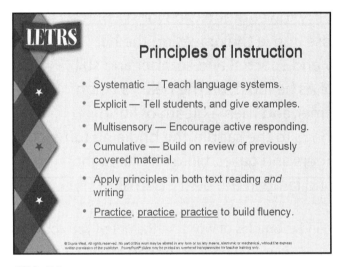

Slide 74

Word study in which students look and listen closely to the internal details of words and sense of word structure will help them read, write, and use those words. Effective instruction is systematic: it proceeds through a defined sequence that follows a continuum of complexity from easy to difficult. It is not "drill and kill"; rather, it combines insight into word structure with meaningful practice.

Multisensory, active learning techniques hold students' attention. Activities for word study should involve touching or moving objects such as index cards or letter tiles; using gestures; incorporating rhythm; tracking with a pencil; and saying words as they are being read or written. Decoding and word analysis comprise only one component of a complete reading lesson that includes fluency building, vocabulary development, and reading comprehension in a variety of texts. Given such instruction, most students can become able readers.

The Content of Decoding and Word Study Lesson

LETRS

Summary: Lesson Content

- Define the concept (sound, spelling, syllable, morpheme).
- Teach phoneme-grapheme correspondence.
- Analyze by syllables.
- Read whole words, blend syllables.
- Study morpheme structure and word origin.
- Build fluency — Add speed drills (brief!), if needed.
- Spell and write to dictation.
- Incorporate daily text reading, using the words learned.

© Sopris West. All rights reserved. No part of this work may be altered in any form or by any means, electronic or mechanical, without the express written permission of the publisher. PowerPoint® slides may be printed as overhead transparencies for teacher training only.

Slide 75

Readers who struggle with reading fluency and word recognition are far more likely to progress if their instruction moves systematically and explicitly through sound-symbol correspondence, syllable patterns, morphology, and word origin. These levels of language awareness can be taught as interconnected strands, as in the *Spellography* (Moats & Rosow, 2002) and *LANGUAGE!*© (Fell Greene, 2000) programs. Vocabulary of interest to older students can be used to teach concepts about language structure. If the study of word structure is linked to reading and writing connected text, students are likely to understand why they are studying the building blocks. Recommended segments in the word study part of a reading lesson include:

♦ Concept definition (identification of a sound, syllable pattern, morpheme, etc.)

♦ Phoneme-grapheme mapping

♦ Syllable analysis, sorting, combining

♦ Reading whole words by tracking syllables

♦ Morpheme study—prefixes, suffixes, roots, and word origin

♦ Fluency-building drills, games, routines

♦ Spelling and writing to dictation

♦ Daily text reading in which the lesson is applied.

Retake the Pretest (page 4) if you have not already checked yourself!

Posttest

Read this passage first (Black Beauty, a horse, is narrating this story):[11]

One day late in the autumn, my master had a long journey to go on business. I was put into the dog-cart, and John went with his master. I always liked to go in the dog-cart, it was so light, and the high wheels ran along so pleasantly. There had been a great deal of rain and now the wind was very high, and blew the dry leaves across the road in a shower. We went along merrily till we came to the toll-bar and the low wooden bridge. The river banks were rather high, and the bridge, instead of rising, went across just level, so that in the middle, if the river was full, the water would be nearly up to the woodwork and planks; but as there were good substantial rails on each side, people did not mind it.

The man at the gate said the river was rising fast, and he feared it would be a bad night. Many of the meadows were under water, and in one low part of the road the water was half way up to my knees; the bottom was good, and the master drove gently …

A teacher might select the words below for previewing or word study. Identify a few critical features of each word (phoneme-grapheme correspondence; letter sequences; syllable patterns; morphology; word origin) that can be taught explicitly during word study.

autumn	level	business	rising	merrily
journey	substantial	pleasantly	gently	bottom

[11] Sewell, A. (originally published in 1877). (2002). *Black beauty* (Reissue ed.) (p. 46). New York: Signet Classics.

Bibliography

Adams, M.J., Treiman, R., & Pressley, M. (1997). Reading, writing, and literacy. In I. Sigel & A. Renninger (Eds.), *Handbook of child psychology, Volume 4: Child psychology in practice* (pp. 275–276). New York: Wiley.

American Federation of Teachers. (1999). *Teaching reading is rocket science.* Washington, DC: Author.

This is a proposal by the AFT to have all teacher candidates learn about the structure of language, the basics of reading psychology, the implementation of research-based practices, and the procedures of valid assessment.

Archer, A.L., Gleason, M.M., & Vachon, V.L. (2003). Decoding and fluency: Foundation skills for struggling older readers. *Learning Disability Quarterly, 26,* 89–101.

Armbruster, B., Osborn, J., & Lehr, F. (2001). *Put reading first.* Washington, DC: National Institute for Literacy.

A clearly written and beautifully produced summary of the National Reading Panel's recommendations on early-reading instruction, for teachers and other educators interested in applying the guidelines and requirements of the Reading First legislation. *Put Reading First* is distributed by the National Institute for Literacy and published by the U.S. Department of Education.

Berninger, V., Nagy, W., Carlisle, J., Thomson, J., Hoffer, D., Abbott, S., Abbott, R., Richards, T., & Aylward, E. (2003). Effective treatment for children with dyslexia in grades 4–6: Behavioral and brain evidence. In B. Foorman (Ed.), *Preventing and remediating reading difficulties: Bringing science to scale* (pp. 275–297). Timonium, MD: York Press.

Bickart, T. (1998). *Preventing reading difficulties in young children* (Summary Report, National Academy of Sciences). U.S. Department of Education.

This is a layperson's version of the National Academy of Sciences' consensus report on prevention of reading failure by Snow, Burns, and Griffin, 1998.

Carlisle, J. (1995) Morphological awareness and early reading achievement. In L.B. Feldman (Ed.), *Morphological aspects of language processing* (pp. 189–210). Hillsdale, NJ: Erlbaum.

Chomsky, C. (1970). Reading, spelling, and phonology. *Harvard Educational Review, 40*(2), 287–309.

Curtis, M.E. (2002). *Adolescent reading: A synthesis of research.* The Partnership for Reading. Retrieved August 13, 2004, from http://216.26.160.105/conf/nichd/synthesis.asp.

Eden, G. & Moats, L.C. (2002). The role of neuroscience in the remediation of students with dyslexia. *Nature Neuroscience, 5,* 1080–1084.

Ehri, L. (1998). Grapheme-phoneme knowledge is essential for learning to read words in English. In J. Metsala & L. Ehri (Eds.), *Word recognition in beginning literacy* (pp. 3–40). Mahwah, NJ: Erlbaum.

Ehri, L.C. & Soffer, A.G. (1999). Graphophonemic awareness: Development in elementary students. *Scientific Studies of Reading, 3,* 1–30.

Fletcher, J. & Lyon, G.R. (1998). Reading: A research-based approach. In W. Evers (Ed.), *What's gone wrong in America's classrooms?* (pp. 49–90). Stanford, CA: Hoover Institution Press.

Foorman, B.R., Chen, D.T., Carlson, C., Moats, L., Francis, D.J., & Fletcher, J.M. (2003). The necessity of the alphabetic principle to phonemic awareness instruction. *Reading and Writing, 16,* 289–324.

Gough, P.B., Juel, C., & Griffith, P. (1992). Reading, spelling, and the orthographic cipher. In P. Gough, L. Ehri, & R. Treiman (Eds.), *Reading acquisition* (pp. 18–48). Hillsdale, NJ: Erlbaum.

Henry, M. (2003). Unlocking literacy: *Effective decoding and spelling instruction.* Baltimore: Paul Brookes Publishing.

Juel, C. (1994). *Learning to read and write in one elementary school.* New York: Springer-Verlag.

King, D. (2000). *English isn't crazy: The elements of our language and how to teach them.* Baltimore: York Press.

Learning First Alliance. (1998). *Every child reading: An action plan.* Washington, DC: Author.

A consensus report from 12 educational leadership organizations on scientifically based early-reading instruction.

Learning First Alliance. (2000). *Every child reading: A professional development guide.* Washington, DC: Author.

A consensus report from 12 educational leadership organizations on the implications of scientifically based early-reading instruction for the professional development of teachers that discusses the context, content, and process of training teachers.

Moats, L. (2001). When older kids can't read. *Educational Leadership, 58*(6), 36–40.

National Institute of Child Health and Human Development. (2000). *Teaching children to read: An evidence-based assessment of the scientific research literature on reading and its implications for reading instruction* (Summary Report, National Reading Panel). Washington, DC: Author.

The lengthier report and its summary can be obtained from the Web site www.nationalreadingpanel.org/Publications/summary.htm (retrieved October 6, 2004). This report is the work of a blue-ribbon panel that reviewed scientifically credible reading research, meta-analyzed the findings regarding the instruction of the components of reading, and issued recommendations that form the basis of the Reading First legislation.

National Reading Panel. (2000). *Teaching children to read: An evidence-based assessment of the scientific research literature on reading and its implications for reading instruction* (Summary Report). Washington, DC: National Institute of Child Health and Human Development.

Rayner, K., Foorman, B.F., Perfetti, C.A., Pesetsky, D., & Seidenberg, M.S. (2001). How psychological science informs the teaching of reading. *Psychological Science in the Public Interest, 2*(2), 31–74.

Rashotte, C.A., MacPhee, K., & Torgesen, J.K. (2001). The effectiveness of a group reading instruction program with poor readers in multiple grades. *Learning Disability Quarterly, 24,* 119–134.

Scheerer-Neumann, G. (1981). The utilization of intraword structure in poor readers: Experimental evidence and a training program. *Psychological Research, 43,* 155–178.

Shankweiler, D., Crane, S., Katz, L., Fowler, A.E., Liberman, A.M., Brady, S.A., Thornton, R., Lindquist, E., Dreyer, L., Fletcher, J.M., Stuebing, K.K., Shaywitz, S.E, & Shaywitz, B.A. (1995). Cognitive profiles of reading-disabled children: Comparison of language skills in phonology, morphology, and syntax. *Psychological Science, 6,* 149–56.

Shankweiler, D., Lundquist, E., Dreyer, L.G., & Dickinson, C.C. (1996). Reading and spelling difficulties in high school students: Causes and consequences. *Reading and Writing: An Interdisciplinary Journal, 8,* 267–294.

Shankweiler, D., Lundquist, E., Katz, L., Stuebing, K.K., Fletcher, J.M., Brady, S., Fowler, A., Dreyer, L.G., Marchione, K.E., Shaywitz, S.E., & Shaywitz, B.A. (1999). Comprehension and decoding: Patterns of association in children with reading difficulties. (Connecticut Longitudinal Study.) *Scientific Studies of Reading, 31,* 69–94.

Share, D.L. & Stanovich, K.E. (1995). Cognitive processes in early reading development: Accommodating individual differences into a model of acquisition. *Issues in Education: Contributions from Educational Psychology, 1,* 1–57.

Stanovich, K.E. (2001). *Progress in understanding reading: Scientific foundations and new frontiers.* New York: Guilford.

Torgesen, J.K., Alexander, A.W., Wagner, R.K., Rashotte, C.A., Voeller, K., Conway, T., & Rose, E. (2001). Intensive remedial instruction for children with severe reading disabilities: Immediate and long-term outcomes from two instructional approaches. *Journal of Learning Disabilities, 34,* 33–58.

Torgesen, J.K., Rashotte, C., Alexander, A., Alexander, J., & MacPhee, K. (2003). Progress toward understanding conditions necessary for remediating reading difficulties in older children. In B. Foorman (Ed.), *Preventing and remediating reading difficulties: Bringing science to scale* (pp. 275–297). Timonium, MD: York Press.

Instructional Resources

Archer, A.L., Gleason, M.M., & Vachon, V.L. (2003). *Rewards.* Longmont, CO: Sopris West Educational Services.

Archer, A.L., Gleason, M.M., & Vachon, V.L. (2003). *Rewards Plus.* Longmont, CO: Sopris West Educational Services.

Bear, D.R., Invernizzi, M., Templeton, S., & Johnson, F. (2003). *Words their way* (3rd ed.). Upper Saddle River, NJ: Merrill.

Bebko, A.R., Alexander, J., & Doucet, R. (1998). *LANGUAGE! Roots* (1st ed.). Longmont, CO: Sopris West Educational Services.

Birsh, J. (Ed). (1999). *Multisensory teaching of basic language skill.* Baltimore: Paul Brookes Publishing.

Ebbers, S. (2004). *Vocabulary through morphemes: Suffixes, prefixes, and roots for the intermediate grades.* Longmont, CO: Sopris West Educational Services.

Ganske, K. (2001). *Word journeys.* New York: Guilford Press.

Grace, K. (in press). *Linking sounds to print: Phonics rescue with phoneme-grapheme mapping* (working title). Longmont, CO: Sopris West Educational Services.

Greene, J. F. (2000). *LANGUAGE!* (2nd ed.). Longmont, CO: Sopris West Educational Services.

Henry, M. (2003). *Unlocking literacy: Effective decoding and spelling instruction.* Baltimore: Paul Brookes Publishing.

Henry, M.K. & Redding, N.C. (1996). *Patterns for success in reading and spelling.* Austin, TX: Pro-Ed.

Johnson, K. & Bayrd, P. (1998). *Megawords.* Cambridge, MA: Educators Publishing Service.

Jones, T.B. (1997). *Decoding and encoding English words.* Timonium, MD: York Press.

Lederer, R.R. (1987). *Anguished English: An anthology of accidental assaults upon our language.* Charleston, SC: Wyrick & Company.

MacPhee, K. (1998). *SpellRead P.A.T.* Charlottetown, Canada: SpellRead P.A.T. Learning Systems, Inc.

Minsky, M. (2002). *The Greenwood word lists.* Longmont, CO: Sopris West Educational Services.

Moats, L.C. & Rosow, B. (2002). *Spellography.* Longmont, CO: Sopris West Educational Services.

Shefelbine, J. & Newman, K.K. (2000). *Systematic instruction in phoneme awareness phonics, and sight words (SIPPS).* Oakland, CA: Developmental Studies Center.

Sonday, A. (1997). *The Sonday system.* St. Paul, MN: Winsor Learning, Inc.

Glossary

affix: a morpheme or meaningful part of a word attached before or after a root to modify its meaning; a category that subsumes prefixes, suffixes, and infixes

alphabetic principle: the principle that letters are used to represent individual phonemes in the spoken word; a critical insight for beginning reading and spelling

alphabetic writing system: a system of symbols that represent each consonant and vowel sound in a language

Anglo-Saxon: Old English; a Germanic language spoken in Britain before the invasion of the Norman French in 1066

base word: a free morpheme to which affixes can be added, usually of Anglo-Saxon origin

closed syllable: a written syllable containing a single vowel letter that ends in one or more consonants; the vowel sound is short

concept: an idea that links other facts, words, and ideas together into a coherent whole

conjunction: a word that connects a dependent clause to a dependent clause, or a word that connects two independent clauses

consonant: a phoneme (speech sound) that is not a vowel, and that is formed with obstruction of the flow of air with the teeth, lips, or tongue; also called a closed sound in some instructional programs; English has 40 or more consonants

consonant blend: two or three adjacent consonants before or after the vowel in a syllable (e.g., **st-**, **spr-**, **-lk**, **-mp**)

consonant digraph: a letter combination that represents one speech sound that is not represented by either letter alone (e.g., **sh**, **th**, **wh**, **ph**, **ch**, **ng**)

Consonant -le syllable: a written syllable found at the ends of words such as *paddle*, *single*, and *rubble*

cumulative instruction: teaching that proceeds in additive steps, building on what was previously taught

decodable text: text in which a high proportion of words (80%–90%) comprise sound-symbol relationships that have already been taught; used for the purpose of providing practice with specific decoding skills; a bridge between learning phonics and the application of phonics in independent reading of text

decoding: the ability to translate a word from print to speech, usually by employing knowledge of sound-symbol correspondences; also the act of deciphering a new word by sounding it out

dialects: mutually intelligible versions of the same language with systematic differences in phonology, word use, and/or grammatical rules

dictation: the teacher repeats words, phrases, or sentences slowly while the children practice writing them accurately

digraph: (see consonant digraph)

diphthong: a vowel produced by the tongue shifting position during articulation; a vowel that feels as if it has two parts, especially the vowels spelled **ou** and **oi**. Some linguistics texts also classify all tense (long) vowels as diphthongs

direct instruction: the teacher defines and teaches a concept, guides children through its application, and arranges for extended guided practice until mastery is achieved

dyslexia: an impairment of reading accuracy and fluency attributable to an underlying phonological processing problem, usually associated with other kinds of language processing difficulties

generalization: a pattern in the spelling system that generalizes to a substantial family of words

grapheme: a letter or letter combination that spells a phoneme; can be one, two, three, or four letters in English (e.g., **e, ei, igh, eigh**)

high-frequency word: a word that occurs very often in written text; a word that is among the 300 to 500 most often used words in English text

inflection: a type of bound morpheme; a grammatical ending that does not change the part of speech of a word but that marks its tense, number, or degree in English (e.g., **-ed, -s, -ing**)

integrated: when lesson components are interwoven and flow smoothly together

irregular word: one that does not follow common phonic patterns; one that is not a member of word family (e.g., *were, was, laugh, been*)

meaning processor: the neural networks that attach meanings to words that have been heard or decoded

morpheme: the smallest meaningful unit of the language

morphology: the study of the meaningful units in the language and how they are combined in word formation

multisyllabic: having more than one syllable

nonsense word: a word that sounds like a real English word and can be sounded out, but that has no assigned meaning (e.g., *lemidation*)

orthographic processor: the neural networks responsible for perceiving, storing, and retrieving the letter sequences in words

orthography: a writing system for representing language

phoneme: a speech sound that combines with others in a language system to make words

phoneme awareness (*also* **phonemic awareness**): the conscious awareness that words are made up of segments of our own speech that are represented with letters in an alphabetic orthography

phoneme-grapheme mapping: an activity for showing how letters and letter combinations correspond to the individual speech sounds in a word

phonics: the study of the relationships between letters and the sounds they represent; also used as a descriptor for code-based instruction in reading (e.g., "the phonics approach" or "phonic reading")

phonological awareness: metalinguistic awareness of all levels of the speech sound system, including word boundaries, stress patterns, syllables, onset-rime units, and phonemes; a more encompassing term than phoneme awareness

phonological processor: a neural network in the frontal and temporal areas of the brain, usually the left cerebral hemisphere, that is specialized for speech-sound perception and memory

phonology: the rule system within a language by which phonemes can be sequenced and uttered to make words

prefix: a morpheme that precedes a root and that contributes to or modifies the meaning of a word; a common linguistic unit in Latin-based words

reading fluency: speed of reading; the ability to read text with sufficient speed to support comprehension

root: a bound morpheme, usually of Latin origin, that cannot stand alone but that is used to form a family of words with related meanings

schwa: the "empty" vowel in an unaccented syllable (e.g., the last syllables of *circus* and *bagel*)

semantics: the study of word and phrase meanings

silent letter spelling: a consonant grapheme with a silent letter and a letter that corresponds to the vocalized sound (e.g., **kn, wr, gn**)

sound blending: saying the individual phonemes in a word, then putting the sounds together to make a whole word

sound-symbol correspondence: same as phoneme-grapheme correspondence; the rules and patterns by which letters and letter combinations represent speech sounds

speed drills: one-minute timed exercises to build fluency in learned skills

stop: a type of consonant that is spoken with one push of breath and not continued or carried out, including / p /, / b /, / t /, / d /, / k /, / g /

structural analysis: the study of affixes, base words, and roots

suffix: a derivational morpheme added to a root or base that often changes the word's part of speech and that modifies its meaning

syllabic consonants: / m /, / n /, / l /, / r / can do the job of a vowel and make an unaccented syllable at the ends of words such as *rhythm, mitten, little,* and *letter*

syllable: the unit of pronunciation that is organized around a vowel; it may or may not have consonants before or after the vowel

vowel: one of a set of 15 vowel phonemes in English, not including vowel-**r** combinations; an open phoneme that is the nucleus of every syllable; classified by tongue position and height (high-low, front-back)

vowel team: graphemes that can represent long vowel sounds, short vowel sounds, or diphthongs (e.g., **ou, oi**); vowel teams can be two letters (e.g., **ai, ea**), three letters (e.g., **igh, eau**), or four letters (e.g., **eigh, ough**)

word family: a group of words that share a rime (a vowel plus the consonants that follow; e.g., **-ame, -ick, -out**)

word recognition: the ability to identify the spoken word that a printed word represents; to name the word on the printed on the page

Appendix A

Answers to Pretest and Applicable Exercises

Pretest: Survey of Word Knowledge for Teachers

Answer the questions on this survey to see how much you already know about the structure of English words. We expect you to be unsure of some answers; that's why this module was written! You'll do the survey again once the module is completed.

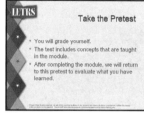

Take the Pretest

* You will grade yourself.
* The test includes concepts that are taught in the module.
* After completing the module, we will return to this pretest to evaluate what you have learned.

Slide 4

1. Identify the letter groups that correspond to each of the speech sounds in the following words. Circle each letter or letter group (grapheme) that corresponds to a speech sound (phoneme).

   (b)(ir)(ch)   (f)(r)(igh)(t)   (w)(a)(t)(ch)   (s)(c)(r)(a)(m)(ble)   (s)(l)(a)(te)   (h)(e)(a)(v)(en)(ly)

2. Divide each of these words into syllables, using syllable division principles to guide pronunciation.

   cooperate   unremitting   comedy   vaccination

   poetry   panorama   slugger   impersonal

3. Sort these words into one of three groups: those that appear to come from Old English (Anglo-Saxon), those that come from Latin, and those that come from Greek. (Label each word AS, L, or Gk on the line before the word.)

   _AS_ water   _GK_ omnivore   _L_ aquarium   _L_ irrigation

   _L_ submersion   _GK_ chlorophyll   _AS_ bread   _AS_ drought

4. Explain the spelling convention that is illustrated by each double-letter pattern in the following words:

   a. floss   _Final s is usually doubled when it s right after a short vowel._

   b. flapped   _Consonant doubling rule when the suffix begins with a vowel_

   c. commit   _Prefix com is added to the root "mit."_

   d. illiterate   _"Chameleon" prefix ill (changed from in) added to the root liter._

◆ Read the novel words in this passage as well as you can:

To stabilize the pretractal fordex, the brave engineer resituated the gyrine. Then he tribled the cabulum.

"Oh, whippers!" he exclaimed. "Thank heavens, I'm no longer befuddled by this problem."

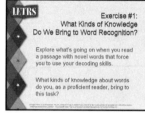

Exercise #1: What Kinds of Knowledge Do We Bring to Word Recognition?

Explore what's going on when you read a passage with novel words that force you to use your decoding skills.

What kinds of knowledge about words do you, as a proficient reader, bring to this task?

Slide 14

◆ Answer these questions:

1. What is the root of the word *pretractal*? How many meaningful parts (morphemes) are there in that word?

   Tract is the root, as in the words retract, contract, and extract. Pre- is the
   prefix, tract is the root, and -al is the suffix. There are three morphemes.

2. Where is the syllable stress or accent in the word *pretractal*? Why?

   Tract is stressed, because it is the root.

3. How did you pronounce the first **t** in the word *resituated*? Why?

   / ch /. The mouth puckers into a / ch / before the / yū / sound; it's the
   consequence of coarticulation, or the spreading of features of one phoneme to
   another when they are juxtaposed.

4. How did you pronounce the word *gyrine*? What other known word might you be comparing it to?

   The most likely pronunciation is "jy-REEN." The g is a soft / j / because it is
   followed by y, as in gyrate. The last syllable can be read by analogy to words
   such as chlorine and pristine.

Exercise #1 *(continued)*

5. Is the vowel in the first syllable of the word *tribled* long or short? Why?

   The vowel is long because the syllable ends in the single vowel and is an open
   syllable. We know that because the -ble goes together as a Consonant-le
   syllable pattern. The analogy is to bible.

6. Where is the accent on the word *befuddled*? Why?

   Accents are not placed on prefixes such as be- or on a final Consonant-le
   syllable. That leaves fud as the accented syllable.

7. What kind of word (i.e., part of speech) is *cabulum*? How do you know?

   It is a noun. It s preceded by an article—the—and it has a standard Latin noun
   ending, as in curriculum and stadium.

8. Is the first vowel in the word *whippers* long or short? Why?

   The vowel is short. The double p must be divided in the middle, leaving the first
   syllable closed by the / p /.

◆ **Discussion:** Consider the various types of word knowledge that allowed you to read the words in this passage. Can you find an instance in which you:

* Made a letter-sound (grapheme-phoneme) association?

  gy = soft g (/ j /)

* Made an analogy between the word parts and patterns of the new word with those of a known word?

  gyrine-chlorine or pristine

* Divided a word into common meaningful parts (morphemes)?

  pre-tract-al

* Applied syllable division conventions to decide how to pronounce a vowel?

  tri-bled: whip-pers

* Recognized a familiar whole word by sight?

  brave, engineer, exclaimed, thank, heavens, longer, problem

---

Exercise #2: Finding Anglo-Saxon, Latin, and Greek in English

◆ Combine these word parts to make as many new words as you can in the table below.

◆ Then decide what language each word probably came from. Use a dictionary if you need to.

Exercise #2: Finding Anglo-Saxon, Latin, and Greek in English

* Build words out of these parts.
* Guess what language they come from!
* You MAY use the dictionary to confirm your guess.
* The Answer Key is in the back of the book (Appendix A).

Slide 26

graph	-ology	dog	phon(e) / phono	audi	xylo	-ed
say	-tory	cep	ear	per		
-tion	shot	listen	-er	hear		

Anglo-Saxon (AS) (Old English)	Latin (L) (Romance)	Greek (Gr)
hearsay	auditory	phonograph
dog-eared	audiology (L/Gr)	xylophone
earshot	perception	phonology
earphone (AS + Gr)		audiology (L/Gr)
listener, listened		graphology
sayer		earphone (AS + Gr)

Exercise #3: Mapping Two Closed Syllables

♦ Write the words using phoneme-grapheme mapping. Underline each sounded vowel; each creates a syllable.

♦ Write the whole word and scoop the syllables after the graphemes are mapped.
(The first two words are broken down for you as examples.)

1. unzip	u	n	z	i	p			
2. strongbox	s	t	r	o	ng	b	o	x
3. catnip	c	a	t	n	i	p		
4. public	p	u	b	l	i	c		
5. nutshell	n	u	t	sh	e	ll		
6. whiplash	wh	i	p	l	a	sh		
7. quicksand	q	u	i	ck	s	a	n	d
8. bankrupt	b	a	n	k	r	u	p	t
9. spendthrift	s	p	e	n	d	th	r	i	f	t

1. unzip   4. public   7. quicksand

2. strongbox   5. nutshell   8. bankrupt

3. catnip   6. whiplash   9. spendthrift

Exercise #4: Multisyllable Words With Open Syllables

♦ Map these open-syllable words on the grid.

♦ Underline the vowels in the open syllables to distinguish them from the "magic" **e** and closed syllables.

1. female   5. dizzy
2. behave   6. frequent
3. polite   7. relax
4. robot   8. microscope

1.	f	e	m	a	l			
2.	b	e	h	a	v			
3.	p	o	l	i	t			
4.	r	o	b	o	t			
5.	d	i	zz	y				
6.	r	e	l	a	x			
7.	f	r	e	q	u	e	n	t
8.	m	i	c	r	o	s	c	o	p

Exercise #5: Vowel Team Syllables

♦ Underline all the vowel teams in the following words.

♦ Check to see if the patterns fit with those in Table 10.4.

maintain	subway	crayon	beefsteak
daylight	highway	tightrope	cyclone
between	disappear	relief	squeamish
snowflake	raincoat	poached	poultry
mushroom	coupon	mildew	shampoo
pewter	Europe	barbecue	woodbox
ointment	rejoined	cowboy	enjoyment
cowboy	destroy	avoid	rejoin
playground	astound	proudly	notebook

Exercise #6: Identifying -**Cle** Syllables

♦ Separate the final -**Cle** syllable in the following words by scooping under it. Then, isolate the vowel sound of the first syllable.

♦ Identify whether the first syllable is closed (C), open (O), VC-**e**, or a vowel team (VT). (Note that a doubled consonant in spelling corresponds to one *spoken* phoneme.)

C frazzle	VT eagle	C fickle
O title	O maple	VT droodle
C battle	C trestle	C muscle
O ogle	O bridle	O scruple
C little	C gentle	C scramble
C/O unstable	VT steeple	C/VT inveigle

Exercise #7: Sorting One-Syllable Words by Syllable Type

♦ Working with a partner, use the grid below to sort these one-syllable words by syllable type.

wait	with	spire	views	rod	large
height	means	when	by	first	he
kite	took	length	take	walk	fields

Closed	-Cle	Open
with	(none in one-syllable	by
when	words)	he
rod		
length		

Vowel Team	Vowel-r	VC-e ("magic" e)
wait	first	kite
height	large	spire
means		take
took		
views		
walk		
fields		

Exercise #7 (continued)

♦ The syllables below are sorted into the chart categories. Combine any number of syllables to make words. (If this is done in a group, each person can take a syllable card—or two—and then find the person with a match that makes a word.)

♦ In the next reading selection, you can find words to make with these syllables:

pub	meth	con	same	e-	doc	mat	light	point
an-	pur	oc-	com	bet	ac-	re-	thun	pre-
prop	ex-	op-	ap-	storm	un-	lish	od	cern
-ness	lect	tor	ter	-ing	-ed	swer	pose	cur
mon	ter	cess	gions	-der	pare	-er	tend	por
tune	suc	-ful	proach					

Closed	-Cle	Open
pub, meth, con, doc, mat,	(none)	e-, re-, pre-
an-, oc-, com, bet, ac-, thun,		
prop, ex-, op-, ap-, un-, lish,		
od, -ness, lect, -ing, -ed,		
mon, cess, tend, suc, -ful		

Vowel Team	Vowel-r	VC-e ("magic" e)
light, point, gions, proach	pur, storm, cern, tor, ter,	same, pose, pare, tune
	swer, cur, ter, -der, -er, por	

Words created by combining syllables:

published	method	concern	sameness	electric	doctor
matter	lightning	pointed	answer	purpose	occur
common	better	access	regions	thunder	prepare
proper	extend	opportune	approach	storm	unsuccessful

Exercise #7 (continued)

This famous excerpt from Ben Franklin's diaries,[5] in which he describes his experiment with flying a kite during a lightning storm to prove that electricity could be harnessed, contains words with the combined syllables.

…The Doctor, having published his method of verifying his hypothesis concerning the sameness of electricity with the matter lightning, was waiting for the erection of a spire in Philadelphia to carry his views into execution, not imagining that a pointed rod of a moderate height could answer the purpose, when it occurred to him that by means of a common kite he could have better access to the regions of thunder than by any spire whatever. Preparing, therefore, a large silk handkerchief and two cross-sticks of a proper length on which to extend it, he took the opportunity of the first approaching thunderstorm to take a walk in the fields, in which there was a shed convenient for his purpose. But, dreading the ridicule which too commonly attends unsuccessful attempts in science, he communicated his intended experiment to nobody but his son who assisted him in raising the kite.

—Written by Joseph Priestley with Ben Franklin's guidance in 1767

⁵ Lemisch, L.J. (Ed.) (1999). *Benjamin Franklin: The autobiography and other writings* (pp. 232–233). New York: Signet Classics.

Exercise #8: Applying Syllable Division Principles

♦ Read this fourth grade passage about an Aleut boy who lives in Alaska and is learning to fish with his family.[7]

♦ Underline the words with two or more syllables that might be used for word study.

♦ After studying the syllable division rules above, find several examples of words that could be used to demonstrate each rule. Write the words in the correct column of the grid, which appears after the passage.

…Alex loves to snack on tamuuq (tah-MOHK), chewy, dry fish. This tamuuq comes from <u>halibut</u>, his <u>favorite</u> fish to catch. But now that the <u>salmon</u> are <u>running</u>, Alex is <u>going</u> <u>fishing</u> for salmon.

He's been <u>waiting</u> for them to <u>return</u>. As young fry, they left the <u>nearby</u> stream to live at sea. To <u>complete</u> their life <u>cycle</u>, they're <u>coming</u> back to the same stream to spawn.

This <u>summer</u>, nine-year-old Alex is <u>finally</u> old <u>enough</u> to help his <u>father</u> set the gill net. Like their Aleut (AL-ee-oot) <u>ancestors</u>, they catch fish to feed their <u>family</u>.

By next morning, the net is full of flapping fish. They are trapped in the <u>almost-invisible</u> mesh of the net as they try to swim past Alex's beach. Alex and his father pull their net. It's time to "pick" fish.

Alex wears gloves to <u>protect</u> his hands not only from the fine mesh of the nets but also from the stings of <u>jellyfish</u>. It's not as much fun as fishing with a line, but there will be time for that later. Now they must <u>finish</u> <u>landing</u> today's catch.

…Alex cleans salmon <u>alongside</u> his father as <u>seagulls</u> watch from afar. He uses the same knife his <u>grandmother's</u> uncle used to skin bears. He cuts <u>filets</u> from one of the fish for <u>dinner</u>. With the <u>others</u>, he cuts off the head, pulls out the guts, and leaves the skin and tails on. They're for the <u>smokehouse</u>. But as the cleaned fish hang outside, <u>uninvited</u> visitors fly in to steal a meal.

…Alex leaves <u>salmon</u> scraps to wash away with the tide and be eaten by <u>scavengers</u>. The gulls swoop down for a fish feast. As always, they eat their <u>favorite</u> part of the salmon first—the eyes.

⁷ McMillan, B. (1996). Salmon summer. In *Traditions*, Houghton Mifflin Reading: The Nation's Choice© Edition (pp. 635–640). Boston: Houghton Mifflin School.

Exercise #8 *(continued)*

VC/CV	VC/CCV VCC/CV	V/CV VC/V	-Cle
sal/mon	com/plete	hal/i/but	cy/cle
sum/mer	a/long/side	fa/vor/ite	
an/ces/tors	grand/moth/er	e/nough	
flap/ping		pro/tect	
		fin/ish	
		scav/en/gers	

Exercise #9: Scooping Under Syllables

♦ Remember this gem? Mark the syllable divisions in the multisyllable words.

♦ Then, practice scooping the syllables with your pencil as you read the words.

To stabilize the pretractal fordex, the brave engineer resituated the gyrine. Then he tribled the cabulum.

"Oh, whippers!" he exclaimed. "Thank heavens, I'm no longer befuddled by this problem."

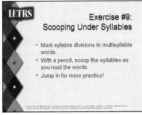

Slide 48

♦ Here's more practice if you need it! Scoop the syllable divisions in the italicized words, using syllable division principles. Show another person how to read those words.

Snow *blindness* is a *temporary* loss of sight caused by bright sunlight *reflected* from snow. It usually lasts from *several* days to a week. *Occasionally*, the person will have trouble *distinguishing* between colors after snow blindness and sees everything colored red for a time. In most cases, snow blindness *disappears* when a person rests the eyes and remains indoors. Wearing *sunglasses* or *goggles* usually *prevents* snow blindness.[10]

[10] Williams, J. (1992). *The weather book* (p. 105). New York: Vintage Books.

Exercise #10: Hearing and Mapping Three Sounds of Past Tense **-ed**

English spelling is "deep" or "morpho-phonological." That means that spelling shows meaningful parts of words even if those spellings do not correspond directly to sound. The first example of this principle is the **-ed** ending.

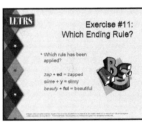

Slide 58

♦ Sort these words in the grid columns by their last sound.

rushed	filled	ended	crossed
invented	asked	dusted	smiled
blazed	wilted	mined	jumped

/ t /	/ d /	/ĭd/
rushed	blazed	invented
asked	filled	wilted
crossed	mined	ended
jumped	smiled	dusted
Possible answer: missed	Possible answer: filtered	Possible answer: spotted
Possible answer: flicked	Possible answer:	Possible answer: wasted
	embezzled	

♦ Add another word or two of your own to each column.

♦ How many syllables are in each word? (Some have more morphemes than they have syllables.) In many past tense words, the morpheme is just a phoneme—not a syllable—as in *begged*, *formed*, *spilled*, and *passed*.

Exercise #11: Which Ending Rule?

Slide 60

♦ Indicate in the third column of this grid the number of the spelling rule that was applied to the new ending of the base word.

Base	Word With Ending	Rule Number
study	studious	3
grime	grimy	2
happen	happened	1b
refer	referral	1b
enjoy	enjoyment	3
peace	peacefully	2

Exercise #12: Suffixes and Syllable Stress

♦ Read these word groups and then put an accent mark over the stressed syllable in each word. (As an example, the first word's stressed syllable letter is bold and underlined.)

♦ Note how the vowel sounds have changed in the different forms of each word.

Slide 65

1. phil**o**sophy
   philosopher
   philosophical

2. diplomat
   diplomacy
   diplomatic

3. nation
   national
   nationality

4. family
   familial
   familiar

Exercise #13: Syllables and Morphemes

♦ Divide each of these words into its morphemes, or meaningful parts. (How to identify a morpheme: 1. You can recognize its meaning; 2. You know other words that use the same morpheme; 3. A dictionary identifies it as one.)

♦ Then, count the number of syllables in the word. (The first two words are broken down as examples.)

Slide 67

Word	Morphemes	Number of Word Syllables
prepare	pre-pare	2
phonograph	phono-graph	3
transferable	trans-fer-able	4
adversity	ad-vers-ity	4
disspell	dis-spell	2
squirmed	squirm-ed	1
irresistible	ir-re-sist-ible	5
pears	pear-s	1
deceived	de-ceive-ed	2
bioluminescence	bio-lumin-esce-ence	6

Exercise #14: Dividing Words by Syllable and Morpheme

♦ Divide these words by syllable and morpheme.

Word	Syllable Division	Morpheme Division
tractor	trac-tor	tract-or
poetry	po-et-ry	poet-ry
unicycle	u-ni-cy-cle	uni-cycle
gentle	gen-tle	gent (le)
underplayed	un-der-played	under-play-ed

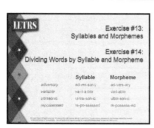

Slide 67

Exercise #15: What Part of Speech?

Derivational suffixes indicate a word's grammatical role or part of speech.

♦ For each word below, indicate whether the word is a noun (**n**), verb (**v**), adjective (**adj**), or adverb (**adv**).

♦ Then, write one more word with another root that has that same suffix.

Slide 68

Word	Part of Speech?	Your Word
national	**adj**	impartial, vertical
nationalist	n	imperialist, socialist
nationalistically	adv	partially, conditionally
nationality	n	fidelity, credibility
nationalize	v	realize, characterize
nationalization	n	fixation, realization
nationally	adv	locally, broadly
nationhood	n	knighthood, personhood
nationless	adj	priceless, formless

Appendix B

Most Common Single-Syllable Rime Patterns, by Syllable Type

Most Common Single-Syllable Rime Patterns, by Syllable Type

Closed	Open	Vowel-r	Vowel Team	VC-e	-Cle	Oddities
ab	**y** (long /ī/)	ar	ail	ace	(not possible in one-syllable words)	all **-ive** (long /ī/)
ack		orn	ain	ade		
ad	**e** (long /ē/)		aw	ake		old
ag			ay	ame		
an	**o** (long /ō/)		eak	are		
amp			eal	ate		
an			eam	ice		
and			ear	ide		
ang			eat	ime		
ank			eed	ive		
ap			eep	(short /ĭ/)		
ash			eet	oke		
at			ew	one		
ed			ight	ope		
ell			ow / ou	ore		
en			oy / oi			
end						
ent						
est						
et						
ick						
id						
ig						
ill						
im						
in						
ind						

Closed	Open	Vowel-r	Vowel Team	VC-e	-Cle	Oddities
ing						
ink						
int						
ip						
it						
ob						
ock						
od						
og						
ong						
op						
ot						
ub						
uck						
uff						
ug						
um						
ump						
un						
ung						
unk						
ush						
ut						

Appendix C

Speech Sounds Charts

 **Module 10**

Reading Big Words: Syllabication and Advanced Decoding

Inventory of Consonant Graphemes

Common spellings (graphemes) for each of the consonant phonemes are listed in the following chart.

Phoneme	Word Examples	Graphemes for Spelling*
/p/	pat, spa, stomp	p
/b/	but, brought, stubble	b
/m/	milk, bomb, autumn	m, mb, mn
/t/	tent, putt, missed	t, tt, ed
/d/	desk, dress, summed	d, ed
/n/	neck, know, gnaw	n, kn, gn
/k/	cot, kettle, deck, chorus, talk, unique, quit	k, c, ck, ch, lk, que, qu
/g/	get, ghost	g, gh
/ng/	rang, dank	ng, n
/f/	staff, asphalt, rough, half	f, ff, ph, gh, lf
/v/	very, give	v, ve
/s/	suit, pass, scent, psycho	s, ss, sc, ps
/z/	Zen, fuzz, rise, his, xylophone	z, zz, se, s, x
/th/	thing, bath, ether	th
/<u>th</u>/	that, seethe, weather	th
/sh/	shawl, pressure, sugar, chagrin, conscious, spatial, mission, special	sh, ss, s, ch, sc, ti, si, ci
/zh/	measure, seizure, vision, rouge	s, z, si, -ge
/ch/	cheese, sketch, (furniture)	ch, tch, (tu)
/j/	judge, page	j, dge, ge
/l/	lice, pill, bubble	l, ll, le
/r/	rat, wrist, under, dirt, surface	r, wr, er/ir/ur
/y/	your, Europe, union	y, (u, eu), i
/w/	want, question, once	w, (q)u, (w)o
/wh/	whale	wh
/h/	harm, whose	h, wh

*Note: Graphemes are spellings for individual phonemes. The graphemes in the word list are among the most common spellings, but the list *does not* include all possible graphemes for a given consonant. Most graphemes are more than one letter.

 106

Vowel Graphemes

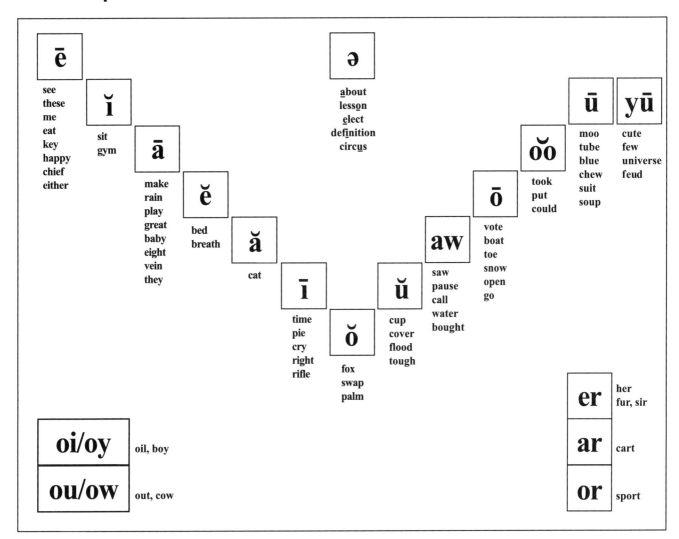